GREATEST SPORTS RIVALRIES

★ 25 OF THE MOST INTENSE *and* HISTORIC BATTLES EVER ★

BY JAMES BUCKLEY JR. & DAVID FISCHER | *foreword by* BILL WALTON

With contributors

TED KEITH, JON SCHER, JOHN WALTERS, JOHN WIEBUSCH *and* ERIC ZWEIG

BARNES
& NOBLE

NEW YORK

MY WORK IN THIS BOOK IS DEDICATED, FOR REASONS THAT WILL BECOME
OBVIOUS, TO THE 2004 BOSTON RED SOX. THANKS, GUYS!
—J.B.

WITH THANKS TO MIKE TORREZ, ALSO FOR OBVIOUS REASONS.
—D.F.

This edition published by Barnes & Noble, Inc., by arrangement with becker&mayer!

2005 Barnes & Noble Books

Copyright © 2005 by Shoreline Publishing Group

M 10 9 8 7 6 5 4 3 2 1

ISBN: 0-7607-7426-9

Design: Kasey Clark and Joanna Price
Editorial: Jenna Land Free
Image Research: Shayna Ian
Production Coordination: Leah Finger
Project Management: Sheila Kamuda

Front cover photos: (top) John Shearer/Time Life Pictures/Getty Images; (bottom) Bruce Bennett Studios/Getty Images
These images have been colorized.

Back cover photos: All Getty Images (top to bottom, left to right) Al Bello; Steve Powell; Rick Stewart; Craig Jones; David Cannon; Doug Pensinger; Karen Levy; Focus on Sport; Focus on Sport; Getty; National Baseball Hall of Fame Library/MLB Photos; Jerome Delay/AFP

Library of Congress Cataloging-in-Publication data is available.

Printed in China.

CONTENTS

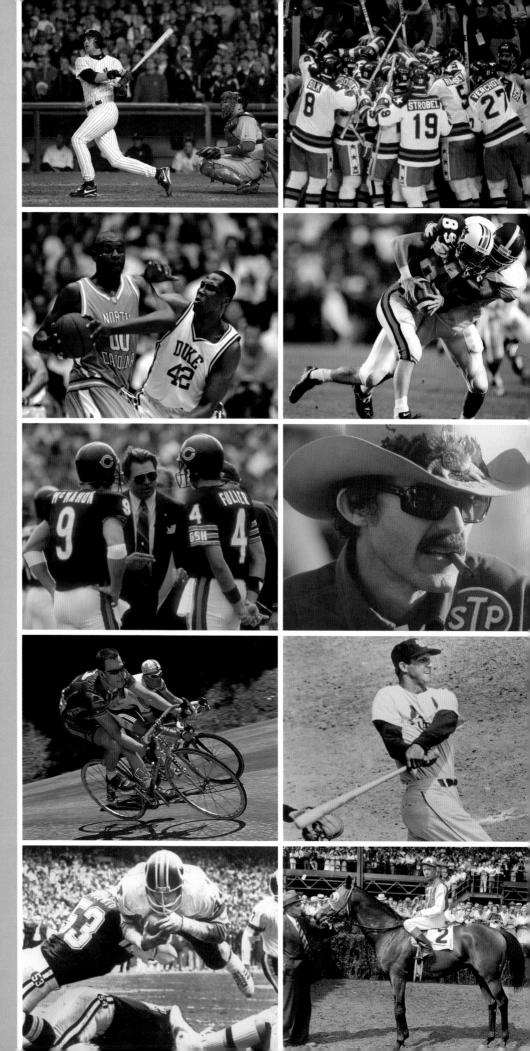

"EVERY TIME YOU WIN, YOU'RE REBORN; WHEN YOU LOSE, YOU DIE A LITTLE."
—GEORGE ALLEN

FOREWORD *by* BILL WALTON

RIVALRIES DEFINE THE TWO MOST EXCITING AND REWARDING ASPECTS OF SPORTS AND COMPETITION: the mental challenge of competing every day, and the emotional response. They're what have always drawn me to sports, but along the way one learns that they're also the hardest parts to conquer and master.

That's because the reason *why* we play is really all that matters.

Rivalries are why it's important to me that UCLA shuts out USC in football, or blows them away in basketball. Rivalries are a major part of why I went to UCLA in the first place—I wanted to play against USC…and to beat them badly. Rivalries are also the reason why when USC plays Notre Dame, I always hope and pray for a scoreless tie.

I grew up watching one of the greatest rivalries of all time: The Boston Celtics versus the Los Angeles Lakers. Even though I was born and raised in San Diego, the heart of Laker country—where it was all Chick Hearn, Jerry West, Elgin Baylor and eventually Wilt Chamberlain all the time—the Boston Celtics were my favorite team, and Bill Russell my favorite player. It seemed like those two teams played every spring to determine not only the NBA Championship, but the fate of western civilization as well.

The Celtics–Lakers rivalry was the driving force in my life as a young boy; it motivated me to excel in sports and drove me to want to be a part of that unique experience. That was my dream. At the end of my line, I had the privilege of playing for my beloved Celtics. We were able to win the NBA title against Houston in 1986, and my dream came true…almost.

I wanted to play the Lakers for the Championship. My whole goal in life was to play against Kareem Abdul-Jabbar in the NBA Finals. Beating the Rockets or anybody else was fine, but I wanted the Lakers and Kareem—because he was *the best*. We *did* get into the Finals again the next year and we did play the Lakers, but I was unable to play because I had yet another broken foot. It might have been the absolute lowest point of my life. My one chance to have all my dreams play out was so close I could feel it, taste it…and then it was gone, and there was nothing I could do about it, ever again.

Sometimes, a match-up feels great even if it isn't a celebrated or historical rivalry. Believe me, I loved every second of beating the Rockets in 1986, just as I loved winning the title in Portland in 1977 when we beat the Philadelphia 76ers. You have to accept in life that the biggest rivalries don't always happen; sometimes the match-ups just don't work out. You can never control who your opponent will be when you're chasing down your dreams.

There are very powerful moments in life where the most important thing is to set a rivalry aside. A few years ago when one of my four sons, Luke Walton, was playing college basketball at the University of Arizona, the Wildcats would regularly play the UCLA Bruins as part of the Pac-10 schedule. As a proud and devoted father, I never missed any of the games Arizona played at UCLA's Pauley Pavilion. Then, when Luke was a junior, Arizona and UCLA were on a collision course in the NCAA Tournament. Over the years, I had been constantly asked how I would deal with that scenario, which team I would pull for. My love and appreciation for UCLA is undeniable, but at the end of every day you want what's best for your children. When you become a parent, your life changes forever, and everything you want becomes subservient to *their* needs. (UCLA lost to Missouri and Arizona lost to Oklahoma, so the match-up never came to be.)

That said, a great rivalry is cause for celebration. It was feeling the love and passion from both sides of a rivalry that drew me into sports when I was a kid. I can still remember sitting in my bedroom with the radio in the mid-1960s, listening as the UCLA quarterback, Gary Beban, led an inspired Bruin team in a remarkable upset of USC at the L.A. Coliseum. It was a defining moment in my life, one of the first of many times where I can remember saying to myself, "that is what I want to do with my life."

Coming of age in the 1960s, it was always the great games of the Dodgers and Giants, the Green Bay Packers and Dallas Cowboys, and the Celtics and Lakers that had that special aura of *the big game*—it sucked me in, and I never wanted to go anywhere else.

Rivalries develop for different reasons. They can be geographic, social, political, economic—or they might be created simply to give you extra motivation on any given day. That emotional push comes from the spark of why you have to win this game, why there's something at stake here. So much of it comes down to that human emotion of pride and what's important to you; why you like somebody, and why you don't. And why it's easier to play against somebody you *don't* like.

As a broadcaster or as a fan, I want to see emotion, I want to see that you care, that this is important. When I'm working, it doesn't matter to me who wins. As a fan, unless it's one of *my* teams, I don't care either. I just want to see the passion, that it matters just how this is all going to play out. When that's the case, *everybody* wins.

It's the same story in every field; it's why the Grateful Dead in the studio are a different band than they are live. Without the passion, commitment and feedback of the fans, it's always going to be a completely different experience. In my own life, there was nothing like playing in Pauley Pavilion and seeing the entire crowd on their feet, screaming at the top of their lungs because the UCLA press wouldn't allow USC to even get the ball up the court. And there was nothing like being in the Portland Memorial Coliseum and hearing the 12,666 Blazermaniacs chanting for the greatest Blazer of them all, Maurice Lucas: "LUUUUUUUKE!" And then in the Boston Garden, there was nothing like the Celtics beating the Lakers, with Larry Bird on fire and the crowd rhythmically pounding out: "Lar-ry, Lar-ry, Lar-ry.... MVP...MVP....MVP!" Once you've been *there*, there is no turning back.

A lot of great things have come my way both on and off the court of my dreams. While my ride has been an epic journey of surreal swings on the wildest roller coaster, in the end it was the rivalries that made it all so worthwhile—where it wasn't just that you won, but who you beat. Sadly, endless injuries kept me out of the game far too often. The frustration, disappointment and embarrassment have left indelible scars—a stain, really—in that I didn't get what I really wanted. But near the end of the line, the people of New England, the Celtics, Red Auerbach, and Larry Bird all gave me a chance...a chance to sit on the bench and be a part of a special team one last time. And while it would be simple to say that they gave me my career back—the real story is that they gave me my life back...and I got what I needed.

—BILL WALTON

INTRODUCTION

RIVALRIES HAVE BEEN A PART OF HUMAN HISTORY FOR MILLENNIA. CAIN WASN'T EXACTLY ABEL'S RUNNING buddy. Scottish clans started hating each other's kilts two thousand years ago, and some of them are still annoyed. The Crusades were one interminably long rivalry. Our nation was founded on a rivalry; I know we were all rooting for the home team in that one. Down South, the Hatfields and McCoys called it a feud, but you could have called it a rivalry with grits. Back in the big world, after World War II, the ultimate rivalry was East vs. West. Someday, maybe it'll be Earth vs. Andromeda.

Sports, of course, is just one of many areas of human endeavor, so it's no surprise that you can find rivalries just about everywhere you look on fields, courts, tracks, diamonds, rings, and other such places. They say the first automobile race came the day the *second* car was built. A football game with one team is a forfeit. You can't box yourself. A one-horse race may be a cliché, but it's also boring.

In fact, there is rivalry in every sporting competition; on any given day, your rival is the team or athlete opposite you. But the rivalries we celebrate in this book are those that surpass a mere meeting of athletes, those that go beyond a simple questing for a single victory. The rivalries in this book (with one obvious one-event exception) are those for whom each meeting is another chapter in a long story. Rather than simply meeting and parting, never to face off again, these athletes are each a link in unbroken chains that stretch over time. Some of those times are briefer than others: Muhammad Ali and Joe Frazier fought but three times in the course of four years, but their match-ups were so intense that theirs remains the most famous of boxing rivalries. Some rivalries stretch through parts of three centuries: The football teams from Army and Navy began playing before the Spanish-American War and continue today, through the second war in Iraq.

Long or short, however, the rivalries featured in this book exude spirit, intensity, ferocity, emotion. It's not enough that the Boston Red Sox finally won their long-awaited World Series in 2004, it's that they finally overcame their seemingly Sissyphean foe, the New York Yankees, on the way to their title. It's not enough that a top college coach like Ohio State's John Cooper put together a dozen years of outstanding success; by failing to dominate against archrival Michigan, he cost himself a job. In many cases, America's Olympic athletes were doing more than just going for medals; they were fighting a battle beyond the sidelines when they faced Olympians from the Soviet Union and East Germany.

Several common elements can be found in most of sports' greatest rivalries. Time, as noted, is one. A college football match-up like Miami and Florida State, which has flourished in the past 20 years, might be considered on some lists of great rivalries, but compared to six decades of debate over Auburn and Alabama, for instance, it doesn't compare. Loyalty is important, especially in college and pro team sports. The players change, the coaches move in and out, the teams might even move (Dodgers vs. Giants, for example), but the rivalries remain fixed in the hearts, minds, and memories of the fans. Jerry Seinfeld joked that with all the player-switching in modern pro sports (and he might have added all the defections by underclassmen from college to the pros) and all the subsequent uniform changes, we're actually just "rooting for laundry." But the joke's on him, because, yes, we *are* cheering for those laundered uniforms, and proudly. So in the greatest of rivalries, look for fans' devotion, even in the face of constant failure (another example from the Red Sox–Yankees rivalry).

Intensity counts big as well. When you hear the players say they pretty much hate the other team, as you might have heard from the Lakers and Celtics across two decades or from the Bears and Packers across seven, then you know you've got a decent rivalry going.

Finally, a rivalry's impact on the historical record plays a part. Williams College and Amherst College have been meeting on the football field every year since 1884, but since they're lacking some of the intensity (are they too nice to hate each other?) and because, frankly, they've never met to determine the top college football team in the land, they didn't make our list. On the other hand, the Notre Dame vs. USC rivalry has an almost tangible aura of historical importance. Their games have featured many of the most talented players in college football history, as well as some of the greatest teams; the pair won 19 national championships between them, by far the most of any pair of college rivals. The names from their games echo through the decades: Rockne, Parseghian, Davis, Holtz, Montana—all of them a part of a rivalry that combines historic import with historic event perhaps more than any other.

So take intensity, loyalty, history, and mix over time, and you have rivalries of surpassing importance, and, well, greatness. The box at right gives some sense of the discussion that went into the selection of these particular rivalries. Here's hoping that yours is on the list, and if it's not, then don't make us into your rival. Look instead for a sequel someday. Remember, loyalty plus time is a good thing.

—J.B.

HOW WE PICKED 'EM

One of the greatest things about sports books is that they stir argument and conversation. This one is sure to be no different. While there are certainly a dozen or so rivalries in this book that no general sports fan would disagree deserve to be included, there are just as surely some rivalries that many will think should be here. Certain college football fans (Texas–Oklahoma, Texas–Texas A&M, Cal–Stanford, Florida–Florida State, heck, North Dakota–North Dakota State, etc.) will be among the disappointed in this regard, for instance. Hockey fans looking for Toronto–Montreal will find themselves left out; that's because we decided to include at least one American rival in each duo.

However, one of the beauties of sports rivalries is that they exist in just about every sport, and we wanted to make sure to visit the head-to-head competition in sports such as figure skating, horse racing, and cycling, as well as the major sports. The wheel-to-wheel intensity of Lance Armstrong vs. his German rival Jan Ullrich, for instance, is no less meaningful for its lack of fall leaves, cheerleaders, or waving pennants. Ice skating is a sport of beauty and grace—but its rivalries have as much intensity as those from the tennis court or the golf course (if not more!).

So, let the arguments begin.

RED SOX *vs.* YANKEES

ONE TEAM HAS WON 26 WORLD CHAMPIONSHIPS SINCE 1918. THE OTHER HAS WON ONE. FOR MORE THAN 70 YEARS, one team has defeated the other in every crucial game in which they met, until the latter team finally came through in 2004. One team has excelled in the clutch time and again, creating a level of dominance over time unmatched in any sport. The other seemed to suffer crushing heartbreak after stunning defeat, always finding a way to lose instead of win. One team even sent its best player over to the other side and watched him become the best player in the history of the game—for the enemy.

This is a rivalry? Sounds more like the sixth-grade boys vs. the kindergarten girls. Doesn't a rivalry have to be at least somewhat even over time?

of the A.L. The Sox started as the Pilgrims in 1901, the Yankees as the Highlanders in 1903. Boston was an early champion, winning the first World Series in 1903. They won four more World Series in the years before and during World War I (1912, 1915, 1916, and 1918). They were, it seemed, a dynasty in the making. The Highlanders became the Yankees in 1908, but it didn't help, and they could have just as easily been called the Lowlanders. They were also the patsies that Boston defeated to inaugurate Fenway Park in 1912.

Boston's final three Series wins of that decade came with the help of a portly former Baltimore farmhand who first found fame as a lefty pitcher. He pitched a string of

THIS IS A RIVALRY? DOESN'T A RIVALRY HAVE TO BE AT LEAST SOMEWHAT EVEN OVER TIME?

Fortunately for sports fans across America, the answer is no. Just because the mighty New York Yankees and the star-crossed Boston Red Sox have followed opposite paths of success (until 2004, but more on that later) doesn't mean that their near-century of animosity is any less fierce, any less intense, any less "wicked hahsh."

Though they have always been at odds on the baseball diamond, whether in the American League or, since 1969, in the A.L. East, until recent years, the rivalry between the two clubs was of import mostly to their own equally rabid and obsessed fans. In 2003 and 2004, however, it spilled over like a red tide into the general populace. Baseball's greatest rivalry finally became sports' greatest rivalry.

Both teams have been around since the early days

29 2/3 consecutive World Series scoreless innings to set a record that stood until 1961. But he took up a bat later on and proved to be pretty good with it, too. The former pitcher set the first of his many, many home run records in 1919, slugging 29 to set an all-time record. His name, of course, was George . . . George Ruth.

You might also know him as Babe.

It seemed as if Boston had a rosy baseball future indeed. However, in a move that would be, as historian Thomas Cahill might say, a "hinge" in history, instead of continuing his blossoming career with the BoSox, Ruth was sold to the New York Yankees. Boston owner Harry Frazee had perhaps solved some of his immediate financial concerns, but he had created as well a poltergeist that

SURE, THEY'RE SMILING BEFORE THE GAME: Red Sox legend Ted Williams poses at Fenway Park with a rising star, Yankee Mickey Mantle, 1955.

HIGHLIGHT REEL
★ ★ ★ ★ ★

DiMaggio vs. Williams

Boston's Ted Williams was, by acclamation, the "greatest hitter who ever lived." New York's Joe DiMaggio was, by official baseball fiat, "the greatest living ballplayer." But that was only after they had finished their careers. During their careers, they were, annually, the two best players in the American League (we'll give Willie Mays the National League, and many would give him the overall lead), battling each other every November in the annual MVP voting, just as their two teams often battled in the A.L. standings.

1941-Williams batted .406 (no one has topped .400 since), yet had to settle for second fiddle to DiMaggio's remarkable 56-game hitting streak (no one has done better than 44 since). Joltin' Joe won the MVP. The war interrupted both men's careers, but they dove back in when it was over.

1946-Williams was the MVP and the Sox were in the Series (though they lost).

1947-Williams won the Triple Crown (leading his league in homers, RBI, and batting average), but, stunningly, lost the MVP to DiMaggio, allegedly because some voting writers downgraded the hypersensitive and press-battling "Teddy Ballgame." As great as Williams was on the field, his contentious relationship with a hectoring press would become as much a theme in his career as his stunning hitting achievements.

1949- Williams won the MVP again, but it was a bitter pill to swallow after Boston's final-game collapse gave the Yanks the pennant.

1951- DiMaggio retired after the season. Williams soldiered on, both literally and figuratively (he served his country again during the Korean War), until 1960. He had won six batting titles, a pair of MVP titles, and had set all-time records for on-base percentage that would last until Barry Bonds did his thing in the new millennium. DiMaggio, however, had what Williams wanted as much as anything else: World Series rings . . . one shy of two hands' full.

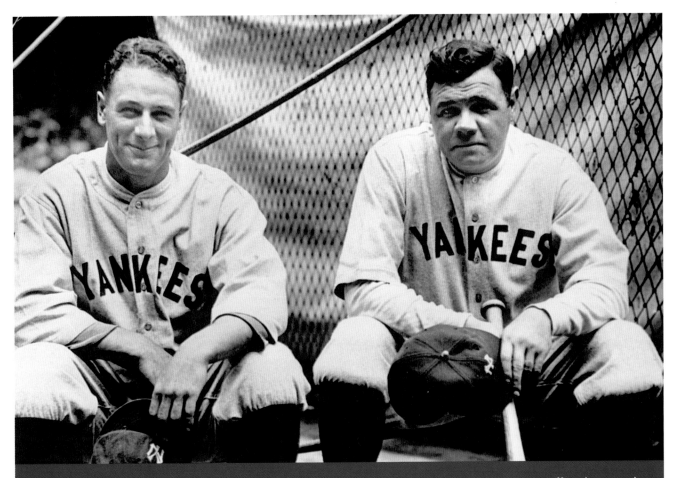

IN THE HOUSE THAT RUTH BUILT: Yankees Lou Gehrig and Babe Ruth, the greatest one-two offensive punch in baseball history, take a rest. This mighty duo led the Yankees to three World Series titles in the 1920s.

would haunt Fenway Park for nearly 90 years: the Curse of the Bambino.

By sending his soon-to-be-fabled star to their interleague rival, Frazee had committed an unpardonable sin. He had, in the opinion of what would become several generations of Boston fans, doomed the team to never win it all again and to be forced to watch their hated enemy succeed. To make matters worse, of course, Ruth and the Yankees simply exploded. The Bambino set record after record while the Yankees won Series after Series. (The Yanks even brought the Red Sox in to play the first game in Yankee Stadium—known as "The House That Ruth Built"— in 1923; the Yanks won, of course.) After winning four World Series titles in seven years through 1918, the Red Sox didn't sniff even a Series appearance until America had defeated Germany (again!) in World War II (during which period the Sox's own enemy in New York won seven World Series).

In those war years, the two teams finally each had

a superstar to call their own: Boston had Ted Williams and New York had Joe DiMaggio (see box). Williams led Boston back to the Series in 1946, but, as they would do three more times in the century, the Sox conspired to lose in seven games, making sure their fans enjoyed as much agony as the rules allowed.

In 1949 the Sox had a chance to put at least some of the Curse to rest in the regular season. They arrived in Yankee Stadium needing to win only one of two games to clinch the A.L. pennant. Of course, they lost both.

Meanwhile, the Sox and the rest of baseball watched in awe as the Yankees again put together a dynasty, winning five straight Series from 1949–53 and adding four more during the years from 1956 through 1962. The rivalry in those years was a wholly one-sided affair.

In 1967 the Yanks were nowhere, for once, and Boston battled into the World Series in their "Impossible Dream" season. Again, they lost the Series in seven games to the Cardinals, who had beaten them in '46.

In 1975 they lost in seven again, this time to the Reds.

In 1986 they lost in seven *again* (this time with the addition of a Game Six comedy of errors that included a hideously timed walk, a passed ball, and, well, an error that took Boston from a strike away from a championship toward yet another agonizing Game Seven loss).

And let's not forget 1978, which came amid that streak of Boston's Series futility. That year, the Sox were cruising, 14 games up on the Bronx Bombers in July. But then Boston watched in horror as the Yanks roared back, pulling off a stunning four-game sweep in Fenway that month, and eventually tying for the A.L. East lead on the last day of the season. For the first time in their long and painful rivalry, the two teams would meet in the postseason—in this case, a one-game playoff to determine the division title.

Decorum prevents me from inscribing here the name,

as Red Sox fans remember him, of the unlikely Yankees home run hero in that single game. Suffice it to say that those around Red Sox Nation are contractually bound to insert a certain Anglo-Saxon adjective between the first and last names of Bucky Dent, just as Yankee fans probably saw an upsurge in "Bucky" babies in the late 1970s.

STARTING IN THE MID 1990s, it looked as if Ruth, DiMaggio, Mickey Mantle, and company were back in the Bronx, as the Yankees crafted yet another dynastic machine, winning four of five World Series from 1996 through 2000. In 1999, thanks to the 1995 addition of a wild-card in baseball, the two ancient and interleague rivals were finally able to meet in the A.L. Championship Series to determine the league champ. Both stadiums were electric with excitement as the rivalry reached its highest peak to that point. The Yankees won the first two games in New York. After the series moved to Boston, former Sox ace

THE YANKEE CLIPPER: Sweet-swinging Yankee slugger Joe DiMaggio connects for another hit, 1945.

STAT BOX

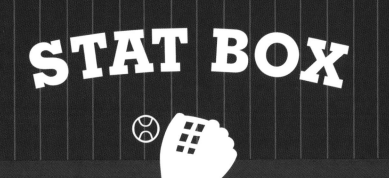

FIRST GAME

MAY 7, 1903

LIFETIME HEAD-TO-HEAD RECORD

YANKEES 1,055–RED SOX 865

WORLD SERIES TITLES

RED SOX: 6

1903, 1912, 1915, 1916, 1918, 2004

YANKEES: 26

1923, 1927, 1928, 1932, 1936, 1937, 1938, 1939, 1941, 1943, 1947, 1949, 1950, 1951, 1952, 1953, 1956, 1958, 1961, 1962, 1977, 1978, 1996, 1998, 1999, 2000

A.L. PENNANTS

RED SOX 11, YANKEES 39

CAREER HOME RUN LEADERS

RED SOX, TED WILLIAMS, 521 • YANKEES, BABE RUTH, 659

HALL OF FAME MEMBERS*

(*MINIMUM TWO SEASONS)

RED SOX 16, YANKEES 24

ESSENTIAL VOCABULARY

"THE HOUSE THAT RUTH BUILT" = NATURALLY, YANKEE STADIUM

"THE EVIL EMPIRE" = BOSTON FANS' SLANG FOR THE TEAM IN THE BRONX

"REVERSE THE CURSE" = THE BATTLE CRY OF BOSTON FANS UNTIL 2004

HIGHLIGHT REEL
★ ★ ★ ★ ★

Baseball Battles

The Red Sox and Yankees don't just battle in the standings and square off in the batter's box: Their rivalry has sometimes taken the form of, well, fights. The intensity of feelings surrounding the game has on several memorable occasions spilled out of the box score and into the boxing ring.

1973-A fierce scrum was sparked by opposing catchers Carlton Fisk of Boston and Thurman Munson of New York.

1976-Sox pitcher Bill Lee injured his shoulder and ended his season during a fight with the Yankees.

2003-During Game Three of the ALCS, baseball watched one of the oddest fights in sports, as ancient Don Zimmer, a former Sox manager and then a Yankees coach, charged at Sox ace Pedro Martinez—who pushed the old fella to the grass. Another fight in the same game involved a Sox groundskeeper and two Yankee relievers!

2004-A short but furious shoving match between the Yankees' Alex Rodriguez and the Sox's Jason Varitek was so emblematic of the rivalry and the season that publishers chose it as the cover photo for *Faithful*, Stephen King's treatise on the season.

Roger Clemens, who had defected to what Boston fans called "the Evil Empire" in the Bronx, faced off against current Red Sox ace Pedro Martinez in Game Three. Boston whomped their once-beloved "Rajah" in that game, but the Yanks came back to win the series. They danced with the Bambino on the Fenway infield on their way to yet another World Series crown.

This Curse thing, thought Boston fans, was getting out of hand.

In 2003 the teams again met with a pennant on the line in the ALCS. For the fifth of six consecutive seasons, the Yankees finished first in the A.L. East, while Boston finished second. Boston fans could only sigh, "So what else is new?" Boston again proved to be a perpetual tease while the Yankees proved again to be the heroic force for good their followers claimed them to be. In Game Seven, the Sox were up by two with five outs to play. But New York got men on and, amazingly, Boston manager Grady Little left a tiring Martinez in the game. The Yanks got four hits off Pedro and tied the game at 5–5. Three innings later, the Yankee faithful watched with unbridled glee as Aaron Boone slugged an 11th-inning leadoff homer to send New York to its 39th A.L. pennant. And the Babe chuckled into his beer . . . again.

The Yankees even managed to win in the off-season. Boston had made a trade offer to the Texas Rangers, along with a contract offer, to obtain superstar shortstop Alex Rodriguez. But the baseball players' union would not approve the new contract, which called for A-Rod to take a (relatively) small pay cut. So in swooped the Yankees, sending their own star second baseman Alfonso Soriano, among others, to Texas for A-Rod, who moved to third base to accommodate the Yankees star at short, Derek Jeter. Shades of Harry Frazee in the baseball transaction business, thought Boston.

Then, in 2004, all hell broke loose. Curses died. Demons were vanquished. And, yet, to many people's surprise, the earth did not spin off its axis into the sun. Yes, it was true, Virginia, there was a Santa Claus. The Boston Red Sox became World Series champions. And, to make it all just achingly perfect, they beat the Yankees on their way there.

But they didn't just beat them. They *historically* beat them. Trailing the Yanks three games to none in the ALCS, Boston faced its final two outs in the ninth in Game

ENDING A LONG NIGHT: Aaron Boone hits an 11th inning home run off Red Sox pitcher Tim Wakefield, sending New York to its 39th A.L. pennant, 2003.

Four . . . in Yankee Stadium . . . against Mariano Rivera, the greatest postseason closer in history . . . staring the Curse in the face once again . . . and came back to tie then win that game. They then proceeded to win the next three games as well, including the final two at Yankee Stadium, in the belly of the beast. The Sox thus became the first team in the sport's history to come back from a 3–0 deficit; more importantly, they made the Yankees the first team to lose four straight after leading a series three games to none.

That the Red Sox then went on to sweep the St. Louis Cardinals in four straight to thoroughly swamp the Curse seemed almost anticlimactic. In fact, some writers wondered whether it would have truly been a Curse-lifting season had Boston won the Series, but not gone through the Yankees to do it? (Of course, Yankee fans had an easy answer for their team's collapse in the ALCS: 26 vs. 1; i.e. World Series won since 1918.)

Nonetheless, Boston fans were elated that the rivalry—for so long a part of baseball lore but only rarely venturing beyond the diamond—became a national phenomenon. Until the Red Sox finally knocked off their hated rivals in the dramatic 2004 ALCS, Boston outfielder Johnny Damon would never have been on the cover of *Entertainment Weekly* (as he was in April 2005) and Sox catcher Jason Varitek and several other Sox would not have been made over on *Queer Eye for the Straight Guy*. A cottage industry in books about the teams, the season, and the rivalry cropped up, with Boston fan and über-author Stephen King leading the way. One of the books was even put out jointly, in a display of journalistic brotherly love, by the *New York Times* and *Boston Globe*. A movie with a Boston fan as a main character, *Fever Pitch*, got big national press on its spring '05 release.

Both teams started the 2005 season sniping at one another in the newspapers, and their first spring training (spring training!) game was a sellout and a big story.

THE AUTHORS AS RIVALS

FROM FENWAY

Do I really hate the Yankees? Of course. My perfect season is a Red Sox championship and the Yankees going 0–162. My two favorite teams are the Red Sox and whoever is playing the Yankees. But until 2004, my hatred had a bitter edge, a sneering growl caused by endless disappointment and frustration. Objectively, I could put on my journalist's hat and say, sure, they're a pretty good team. But subjectively, I don't care how good Derek Jeter is or how nice Bernie Williams is, they're Yankees and I hope they never win again.

But have I mellowed in the months since we won and they lost? Has the curse of Yankee hatred been lifted by the lifting of another Curse? Well, I'm not going to wish them any luck, but when they stood on the dugout steps and applauded as we (I always say we) got our World Series rings in April 2005, I could not help but be impressed.

I still wanted them to lose, though, that day and every other. I just said it with a smile this time.

—J.B.

FROM THE BRONX

Do I really hate the Red Sox? Why bother? They are merely one of several teams buzzing around like mosquitoes that will inevitably get squashed on the windshield of a pinstriped juggernaut speeding towards its final destination: another World Series championship.

My view of the trailing Red Sox had always been in the rearview mirror—until 2004. I used to pity Red Sox fans, but now I'm glad they finally won so their fans will stop bellyaching about some lame excuse of a curse. Sure, I admit it's fun to crush the Red Sox like a grape, but Yankees fans are only concerned with their own team's fortunes. For us, "wait til next year" is not a slogan, it's a reality. The fact that we took one on the chin in '04 is not more devastating because it occurred against the hated Bostonians than the disappointment of other tough World Series losses of recent memory. So perhaps the occasional bitter defeat is easier to swallow when your children and grandchildren don't have to wait 86 years between titles.

—D.F.

Jeter and Damon posed together (giving each other the fish-eye) on the cover of *Sports Illustrated*'s baseball preview issue. The teams each opened their home seasons at each other's parks, and Boston—giggling, probably, as they did it—handed out its World Series rings while the Yankees stewed in the opposing locker room before an April game.

And so, though the Curse lies dead and buried, the rivalry goes on. Boston fans hate the Yankees and New York fans hate the Red Sox. Where Boston fans for years called out to "reverse the Curse," Yankee fans now exhort their heroes to "revoke the Choke" of the 2004 playoffs. In 2003 and 2004, the two teams played 52 total games: the Yankees won 27, Boston 25. There's

no reason to think that for the next few seasons at least, the story won't be more of the same.

In the stands at Yankee Stadium, fans laughingly parade banners that read "See you in 86 more years." In the bleachers at Fenway, the crowd waves goodbye to the Curse and continues to help sales of MLB licensed merchandise rise and rise. The curse is indeed gone, but the rivalry remains as fresh and intense as ever. Yankee fans have 26 championships, but suffer most recently from the "one that got away." Red Sox fans finally have their World Championship, but it's only good for a year . . . and then they start all over again. And so it goes in sports' greatest and fiercest rivalry.

—J.B.

ELATION IN THE BELLY OF THE BEAST: The Red Sox team celebrates the lifting of the Curse after beating the Yankees in the seventh ALCS game, 2004.

UNITED STATES vs. USSR

SPORTS WRITERS OFTEN LOOK TO THE BATTLEFIELD FOR METAPHORS TO DESCRIBE THE ACTIONS ON THE FIELD, court, or rink—a college football "war," a baseball "battle," a basketball "attack." We write about victory over the enemy and the valiant play of those facing great odds. But those metaphors seemed more apt than usual when joined with the literally world-shaking events that played out between the United States and the Union of Soviet Socialist Republics in the second half of the 20th century. While we leave to others the recollection of the more dangerous and life-threatening battles, here we take some time to look back on how that most toxic of international rivalries played itself out on the fields, rinks, and courts of the world.

The minute World War II ended, the Cold War began, a battle between Soviet desires for expansion and United States anti-Communist fervor. In 1947 diplomat George Kennan, years before ESPN's Dan Patrick used the phrase, essentially said that the United States can never hope to stop the Soviets, but we can try to contain them. We supported embattled foreign governments, we supplied anti-Soviet rebels, we sent money to pro-United States nations, and we fought an international propaganda war. And we tried like

hell to beat them on the athletic field. Defeating the Soviets in sports came to be seen as a defeat of Communism itself.

The initial stirrings of this sports saga came in the second Olympics following WWII's end, when the teams from the Soviet Union began to assert themselves on the international stage. After skipping the 1948 Games, they sent a team to the 1952 Games in Helsinki. The "Iron Curtain" that covered the USSR parted to release a team that was "a total mystery to the world," as shot putter Parry O'Brien said. "For all we knew, they had a guy who could throw the shot 80 feet and another who could high jump nine feet."

The team from the USSR built their own quarters, stayed to themselves . . . and stayed off the medal stand. Their first Olympics since 1918 was scored one for the West, as the United States dominated. It was the last time America would do so for decades. Starting in 1956 in Melbourne, the Soviet "sports machine" won the overall medal count at the Games every year until the boycott of 1984 (see page 28).

America got one back during the 1960 Winter Olympics, when an upstart young ice hockey team

DEFEATING THE SOVIETS IN SPORTS CAME TO BE SEEN AS A DEFEAT OF COMMUNISM ITSELF.

AMERICA'S GAME: Top United States scorer Dwight Jones reaches for the ball in the gold medal match against the Soviets, 1972.

LOVE
CONQUERS
ALL

Though the Iron Curtain countries tried to control the movements of their athletes during the Olympic Games, the spark of romance traveled easily between two worlds. At the 1956 Summer Games, Olga Fiktova, a Czech discus thrower, met Harold Connolly, an American hammer thrower. Love bloomed and the two were later married and lived in the United States, becoming a symbol of peace in a time of frigid battle. Olga Connolly later competed in the Olympics as an American and won five U.S. titles. In 1972 she was chosen by her fellow athletes to carry the American flag in the Opening Ceremonies in Munich.

medal ever awarded, dating back to the sport's debut in the Games in 1936, and had never even lost a game in Olympic play. This history of success made the events of September 10, 1972, even more stunning.

The United States basketball team was then made up of college players only, not the NBA-led "Dream Teams" that began in the 1990s. The Soviet teams, which had been improving through the previous decade, were essentially full-time professionals. Under the Soviet athletic system, athletes were supported, trained, and chosen by the state. While the Americans played a handful of exhibitions leading up to Munich, the team from the USSR had been on the court together more than 400 times.

Both teams romped through early competition, racking up easy victories. They were both 8–0 when they finally met in the gold-medal match on September 10. Sadly, this game was played (some say it should have been canceled) in the bloody shadow of the worst event in Olympic history: the death of 11 Israeli athletes at the hands of Palestinian terrorists five days earlier. However, the Games went on, as did this fateful basketball game. The Soviets jumped out to a 7–0 lead and were up by as many as ten points late in the second half. A very rough game, the older and larger USSR team quite obviously whacked the college kids around. They contrived to have Dwight Jones, the top United States scorer, kicked out after getting him into a fight. Another center, Jim Brewer, got a concussion after being knocked down.

With less than a minute left, the Americans trailed by one. Intercepting a pass, guard Doug Collins drove to the hoop with time ticking away. He was brutally hacked and crashed to the ground. At first, it was thought he could not attempt the free throws, but he sucked it up and made both. For the first time in the game, the United States led 50–49. And then things got very interesting.

After Collins made the second free throw and the Soviets inbounded the ball, the referees stopped the game and ordered the clock reset to three seconds. They were responding to Soviet pleas that they had requested a time-out during Collins' time at the line. So, back everyone went to the court, the ball was inbounded, the horn went off, and the game was over. Or was it? Again, the Soviets battled with the officials, and again, the officials, including international basketball federation president William Jones, gave the Soviets another chance over the vehement objections of the Americans, claiming the clock

won the gold medal over a powerful Soviet squad. It would set up the most famous moment in the rivalry 20 years later. The 1960 Summer Games were held in the shadow of the famous U-2 spy plane incident, in which the Soviets captured a downed American pilot. But the Games went on, with the USSR again claiming overall victory.

ONE SPORT in which the United States continued to excel over its Soviet counterparts was basketball. Invented in the United States, played on playgrounds, in gyms, and in backyards around the nation, hoops was, on the international stage, the most American of games. In fact, the United States had won every Olympic basketball had not been fully reset. The American celebration was short-lived, the teams were led back to the court, and three seconds were put on the clock—again. Given new life (and, essentially, three chances), the Soviets made a length-of-the-court pass to enormous Alexander Belov. He caught the ball, bowled over two defenders, laid the ball in, and the horn sounded—again—this time for good. A protest by the United States team was denied by a special jury (whose five members, it should be pointed out, included three Eastern bloc nations, assuring a majority opinion). To this day, American players have not accepted the silver medals they won in that game, and it remains the most controversial team sport contest in Olympic history.

THE OLYMPICS were proving to be a source for some singular moments of pride for Western athletes, but overall, they were a demonstration of Soviet and Eastern bloc machine athletics. In 1980, however, an American team fashioned what might perhaps be the single most memorable sports event of the 20th century, and certainly of this international rivalry.

Like the 1972 basketball team, the 1980 United States ice hockey team was made not of pros, but of college kids (though more than a dozen members of the team did go on to NHL success). The Soviet team, meanwhile, was a juggernaut, a savvy group of veterans who had played together for years, and who had defeated all comers in international events. The USSR won every hockey gold

JOY OF VICTORY?: A United States team celebrates their 1972 win over the Soviets . . . prematurely, as it turns out.

HIGHLIGHT REEL

★ ★ ★ ★ ★

1972
Gold Medal Basketball
Game Play-by-Play

00:03

Americans trail by 1. Guard Doug Collins intercepts a pass and drives to the hoop, but is fouled. He makes 2 free throws, and the United States leads 50–49.

00:00

Soviets inbound the ball. Time runs out. United States team celebrates.

+ 00:03

Three seconds added to the clock, after Soviets plead that they'd requested a time-out during Collins' time at the line.

00:00

Ball inbounded, horn sounds. Time runs out. United States team celebrates.

+ 00:03

Another Soviet plea to officials, claiming the clock had not been fully reset. The panel of officials agrees to put another three seconds on the clock. Soviets make length-of-court pass to Alexander Belov. Belov catches the ball, bowls over two defenders, lays the ball in. Horn sounds.

00:00

Soviets proclaimed the winners.

WOULD YOU LIKE TO TRY THAT AGAIN?: Alexander Belov scores the winning basket against the United States after three seconds were again added to the clock, 1972.

THE MIRACLE

ON ICE

U.S. HOCKEY PLAYERS WHO LATER PLAYED IN THE NHL

BILL BAKER, 3 seasons (Mtl, Col, Stl, NYR)

NEAL BROTEN, 19 seasons (Minn, Dal, NJ, LA)

DAVE CHRISTIAN, 16 seasons (Wpg, Wash, Bos, StL, Chi)

STEVE CHRISTOFF, 5 seasons (Minn, Calg, LA)

JIM CRAIG, 3 seasons (Atl, Bos, Min)

STEVE JANASZAK, 2 seasons (Min, Col)

MARK JOHNSON, 12 seasons (Pitt, Minn, Hart, StL, NJ)

ROB McCLANAHAN, 5 seasons (Buff, Hart, NYR)

KEN MORROW, 10 seasons (NYI)

JACK O'CALLAHAN, 7 seasons (Chi, NJ)

MARK PAVELICH, 6 seasons (NYR, Minn)

MIKE RAMSEY, 19 seasons (Buffalo, Pitt, Det)

DAVE SILK, 7 seasons (NYR, Bos, Wpg, Det)

Of the Olympians to play in the NHL, only Neal Broten, Dave Christian, Mark Johnson, Ken Morrow, Mark Pavelich, and Mike Ramsey made significant marks in the NHL.

medal from 1956 to 1988—with two exceptions, and 1960 was the first. Here came the second.

Leading the young American team was an amazing coach, Herb Brooks, who used intimidation, fear, and intensity to mold his charges into the force he felt they had to be to win. The physical training he put the team through would pay off again and again as the underdog squad beat the Czechs, Norwegians, and West Germans, all via upset. That brought them face-to-face with the Soviets.

It was a back-and-forth game, with the USSR team taking one-goal leads three times only to see the scrappy Americans come back time and again. A goal by team captain Mike Eruzione made the score 4–3 with less than ten minutes remaining. For anyone watching, it was the longest ten minutes of their lives. Again and again, the Americans, led by goalie Jim Craig, turned back the onslaught of the powerful Soviets. The pro-American crowd in Lake Placid, New York, site of the Games, created a deafening show of support. The long training of the players by Brooks paid off, and the players maintained their focus and discipline amid the madhouse.

Finally, as the seconds ticked down, millions of TV fans heard ABC announcer Al Michaels utter one of the most famous calls in sports history. "Do you believe in miracles?

WORKING FOR AN UPSET: Coach Herb Brooks directs members of his team, 1980.

DO YOU BELIEVE IN MIRACLES?: The underdog United States hockey team celebrates after beating the Soviets, 1980. The United States team went on to win the gold against Finland.

MILLIONS OF TV FANS HEARD ABC ANNOUNCER AL MICHAELS UTTER ONE OF THE MOST FAMOUS CALLS IN SPORTS HISTORY. "DO YOU BELIEVE IN MIRACLES? YES!!"

Yes!!" The underdog kids from Minnesota, Wisconsin, and other such prosaic American states had knocked off the mighty Soviet machine. To this day, watching the end of that game brings tears to the eyes of even the most hard-bitten sports fan. Craig circled the ice draped in an American flag. An impromptu serenade of "God Bless America" echoed into the winning locker room. Several days later, the country watched with further joy as the team knocked off Finland to claim the gold medal. Eruzione smiled for a nation as he called his teammates up to join him on the medal stand.

When the endless end-of-the-century polls were taken in 1999, this game was more often than not cited as the most memorable moment in sports history. There's every chance that it will be at the top of the next list 100 years from now.

The joy of the Winter Games turned quickly sour, however. In the spring of 1980, President Jimmy Carter announced that, in response to the Soviet invasion of Afghanistan in 1979, the United States would not be sending a team to the 1980 Summer Games to be held in Moscow. Sixty-one other countries joined the boycott. For almost 30 years, the Olympics had been an unofficial political battleground; now it was official. Carter had first requested that the Games be moved from Moscow; that request was turned down. American athletes were, for

STAT BOX

MEDALS: SUMMER GAMES

UNITED STATES: 2,219

GOLD: 907

SILVER: 697

BRONZE: 615

USSR: 1,010 (1952–1988)

GOLD: 395

SILVER: 319

BRONZE: 296

MEDALS: WINTER GAMES

UNITED STATES: 191

GOLD: 69

SILVER: 71

BRONZE: 51

USSR: 194 (1956–1988)

GOLD: 78

SILVER: 57

BRONZE: 59

TOP GOLD MEDALISTS
(FROM SOVIET PARTICIPATION ERA)

UNITED STATES

CARL LEWIS, TRACK AND FIELD, 9

MARK SPITZ, SWIMMING, 9

ERIC HEIDEN, SPEEDSKATING, 5

AL OERTER, TRACK AND FIELD, 4

USSR

LARISSA LATYNINA, GYMN., 9

NIKOLAY ANDRIANOV, GYMN., 7

BORIS SHAKLIN, GYMN., 7

LYDIA SKOBLIKOVA, GYMN., 6

the most part, crestfallen. Dozens of careers ended with that pronouncement, their moment of glory taken away by fiat. The 1980 Games, it turned out, were almost a farce, as officials quite obviously favored Soviet athletes. It was, in the words of Olympic historian William Oscar Johnson, "a fiasco."

In 1984 came the payback. The Games were scheduled for Los Angeles, and while it was apparent for some time that they would not be coming, the Soviets waited until May to make the official announcement. Thirteen Warsaw Pact countries joined the boycott. For those four years, the athletic rivalry—though certainly not the political rivalry—between the two great powers was sent for a forced time-out, held hostage by events beyond their control. Without competition from the much-favored Russians and East Germans, Americans did well in some sports where they had not previously won, though, unlike

in 1980, the competition was regarded as fairly judged. Mary Lou Retton became the darling of the Games by winning the first women's gymnastics all-around gold for the United States.

The end of the 1980s saw the end of the Soviet bloc, and with it the end of the United States–Soviet athletic rivalry. Athletically and politically, the rivalry had been crumbling from within and from without for years. While the "evil empire" was spending itself into oblivion, athletes from their "side" spent as much time plotting their defection as their training regimen. Today, Russians and Czechs play in the NHL, Lithuanians and Yugoslavs are in the NBA, and Germans are all on the same teams again. At the Olympics, the United States once again reigns supreme. Today, the metaphors of war used in sports are just that . . . and rarely translate into actual life and death.

—J.B.

"THE MOST MEMORABLE MOMENT IN SPORTS HISTORY": Team USA relishes their triumph over the Soviets, in what many consider the greatest moment in sports, 1980.

ARMY *vs.* NAVY

FOOTBALL IS ABOUT CONFLICT, ABOUT THE TAKING OF TERRITORY, ABOUT LEADERS DIRECTING A GROUP TOWARD A SHARED objective, about tradition. West Point and Annapolis are about training leaders for conflict, about the history of taking territory, and about tradition. So it is only natural that the young men charged with learning the arts of war can find that football provides a perfect opportunity to knock somebody silly.

It's an intensity that's been on view for more than 100 years, each time the football team of the United States Military Academy battles the land forces of the

six Heisman Trophy winners played in the game. In the past three decades, however, the game has lost much of its luster as other colleges have roared ahead, thanks to scholarships, bigger budgets, and more training time. On top of that, the academies have maintained their high academic standards while other schools have been freer to live by the singular mantra, "Football is Life."

Not to say that the West Point–Annapolis match-up doesn't still garner its fair share of attention. Regardless

FOR ALUMNI OF BOTH SCHOOLS, FOR STUDENTS, AND FOR ALL MEMBERS OF THE TWO MILITARY BRANCHES, THERE IS AND ALWAYS WILL BE ONLY ONE GAME EACH YEAR THAT COUNTS.

United States Naval Academy. West Point vs. Annapolis. Cadets vs. Midshipmen. The Long Gray Line. Mr. Inside and Mr. Outside. The very air is thick with tradition, from the stirring pregame march of the two academies' student bodies onto the field and into the stands, to the playing of each school's anthem after the game as thousands of blue- and gray- clad future soldiers stand at attention.

There is no doubt that Army–Navy was the greatest rivalry in American sports 50 years ago. The teams not only brought to each game a storied past, but a scintillating present. In 1944 and 1945, the teams faced off as the top two teams in the nation. From 1944 to 1963,

of the teams' records, the big game is always nationally televised. For alumni of both schools, for students, and for all members of the two military branches, there is and always will be only one game each year that counts, only one rivalry in sports that matters. Beat Army! is the constant cry over the waters of Annapolis; Beat Navy! answer the Cadets in the hallowed halls of West Point.

THE RIVALRY BEGAN in football's infancy. Navy put together some ragtag teams beginning in the 1870s; the first official team was formed in 1879. Football, however, made nary a dent in the Army's busy schedule. By 1890, according to Gene Schorr's *100 Years of Army–Navy Football*, "only three

ON THE BRINK OF WAR: Nearly 100,000 spectators turned out for the 42nd annual Army–Navy game just weeks before Pearl Harbor, 1941.

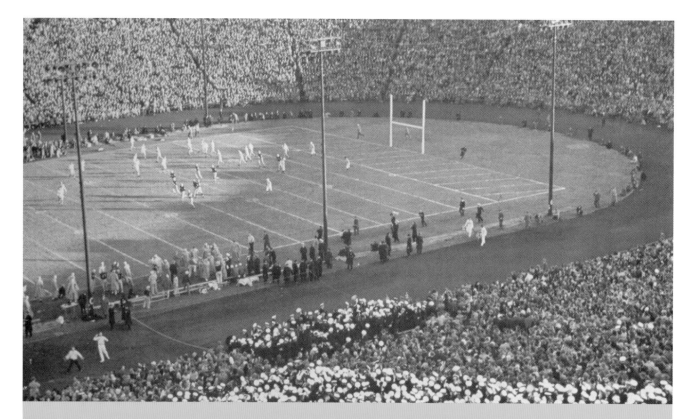

FULL HOUSE: Fans fill Baltimore's Municipal Stadium, 1948. Army was the stronger team in the years immediately following the war, but Navy would soon catch up.

Cadets had ever played an organized football game."

One of that trio was Dennis Michie, and such was his zeal for the sport and West Point (he had been born at the Point as the son of an officer stationed there) that he figured out a way to have Navy challenge Army to a game. Naturally, no such challenge could go unanswered; Army just had to deal with the small matter of actually creating a team to play the established Navy 11.

The game was held on November 29, 1890. While walking to the field, Navy purloined a noisy goat from an Army house; a goat remains the school's football mascot today. It was exciting to get an official game underway,

but a rout. Navy's experience quickly outmatched Army's players. The first score in this great rivalry was earned by Navy, a touchdown by captain Charles "Red" Emerich. Navy not only knew more about the game, they used a system of signals based on nautical and sailing terms, calling out "mainmast" and "reef the topsails," which meant something to them, but nothing to their land-hugging opponents. The final was 24–0, and a storied rivalry was born.

The game was a hit from the start, drawing a crowd of students and alumni, including, according to Schorr, a special seating area for female spectators. The Army–Navy

NAVY NOT ONLY KNEW MORE ABOUT THE GAME, THEY USED A SYSTEM OF SIGNALS BASED ON NAUTICAL AND SAILING TERMS, CALLING OUT "MAINMAST" AND "REEF THE TOPSAILS."

ARMY

NAVY

ARMY	NAVY
BLACK AND GOLD	WHITE AND GOLD
GOLD HELMETS	GOLD HELMETS
MULE (NAMED SCOTTIE)	GOAT (NAMED BILL)
WEST POINT	ANNAPOLIS
LAND	SEA
CADETS	MIDSHIPMEN
BLACK KNIGHTS	MIDDIES
LONG GREY LINE	PUSHUPS AFTER SCORES
GEN. EISENHOWER	ADMIRAL HALSEY
MR. INSIDE AND MR. OUTSIDE	ROGER THE DODGER
"BEAT NAVY!"	"BEAT ARMY!"

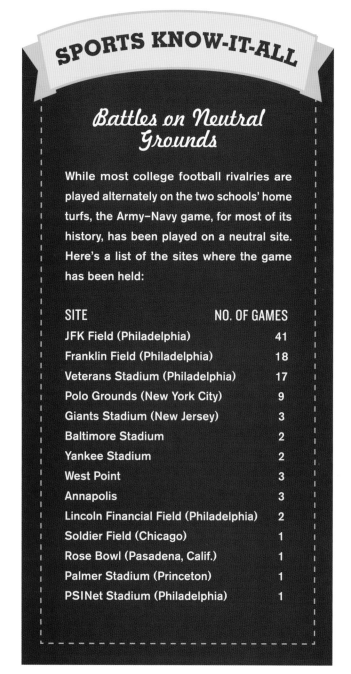

SPORTS KNOW-IT-ALL

Battles on Neutral Grounds

While most college football rivalries are played alternately on the two schools' home turfs, the Army–Navy game, for most of its history, has been played on a neutral site. Here's a list of the sites where the game has been held:

SITE	NO. OF GAMES
JFK Field (Philadelphia)	41
Franklin Field (Philadelphia)	18
Veterans Stadium (Philadelphia)	17
Polo Grounds (New York City)	9
Giants Stadium (New Jersey)	3
Baltimore Stadium	2
Yankee Stadium	2
West Point	3
Annapolis	3
Lincoln Financial Field (Philadelphia)	2
Soldier Field (Chicago)	1
Rose Bowl (Pasadena, Calif.)	1
Palmer Stadium (Princeton)	1
PSINet Stadium (Philadelphia)	1

secretary of the Navy and always a great proponent of the manly benefits of physical activity, wrote a famous letter to Secretary of War (and thus Army chief) Russell Alger urging him to reunite the academy heads and restart the rivalry on the field. In the letter, Roosevelt opined that a player should "not be permitted to join in the training if he was unsatisfactory in any study or conduct . . . and that no drills, exercises, or recitations [be] omitted to give opportunities for practice." In other words, play the game but don't let it get in the way of school. That he was worried about such matters a century ago just shows that the more things change, the more they stay the same.

Roosevelt got his way. Army won the 1899 game 17–5 and the series resumed, almost without pause, for the next century.

A TRAGIC SIDENOTE befell the 1909 season which resulted in one of the few cancellations of the rivalry game. Football before World War I was a brutal affair, home of the flying wedge, the helmetless player, and a pounding ground game that was devastatingly painful. In October 1909, Navy player Earl Wilson died as a result of a neck injury sustained in a game against Villanova. Later that month, Army's popular right tackle Eugene Byrne was knocked out in a game against Harvard and carried off the field. He died the next day.

Army cancelled the rest of its season.

Numerous rules were changed as a result of this tragic season; the two academy deaths were among 14 in college football in that year alone. New rules ended play when a player was down, outlawing piling on. Penalties for incomplete passes were eliminated, helping open up the safer, faster passing game.

Though there were other brief pauses (there were no games in 1917 and 1918 during World War I, and the 1930 and 1931 games were unofficial charity affairs following an eligibility scandal in 1929), the game was firmly established on the sports calendar.

In 1926 what some histories call the greatest game in the history of the rivalry gave the Midshipmen their only national title. The game was played that year in Chicago to inaugurate the city's new Soldier Field. Virtually the entire student bodies of both schools climbed aboard Pullman cars for the ride to Chicago. Army came into the game with but one loss and that to mighty Notre Dame. Navy, meanwhile, boasted perhaps its finest all-around

rivalry was already firmly established in military lore, with each side claiming indispensability when America went out to face its enemies. The rivalry did face some obstacles in continuing, however. Football in those days was a nearly unregulated brawl. The natural enmity of the two academies led to fiercer-than-normal battles, often sparking numerous fistfights and wrestling matches, all without pads. Navy won in 1893 with a score of 6–4, but the game was marked by so much mayhem that President Grover Cleveland banned the contest, a ban which stuck for six years.

A future president was partly responsible for starting the series back up in 1899. Theodore Roosevelt, then team ever; they were undefeated and needed only to win to claim the national title.

An enormous crowd was treated to some great back-and-forth action. In the first half alone, Navy jumped out to a 14–0 lead, only to watch Army score two touchdowns in two minutes just before the half ended, tying the score.

Army's Chris Cagle scored on a brilliant 43-yard run early in the second half to give West Point its first lead. With just four minutes left in the game, Navy intercepted an Army pass and made its final drive. They reached Army territory, and it was soon fourth and goal from the three. Navy called a daring naked reverse; it fooled the overanxious Army defenders, and Alan Shapley scored for Navy. The extra point tied the score. Though not a victory for either team, it clinched a national title for Navy. The exciting nature of play permanently secured

its place as among the greatest games the two teams ever played. In fact, in 1950, the Associated Press called the 21–21 tie the greatest college game of the first half of the 20th century.

During World War II, the Army–Navy game became an annual rallying cry for the millions of servicemen around the world. Radio broadcasts of the game reached the far corners of the European and Asian theaters of war. Navy won the first three wartime games from 1941–1943. But then two players joined Army who would go into history as among the finest college athletes of all time. They had names, of course, but Felix "Doc" Blanchard and Glenn Davis would forever be known as Mr. Inside and Mr. Outside.

Blanchard was a pounding fullback who would win the Heisman Trophy—Army's first—in 1944. Davis was a swift

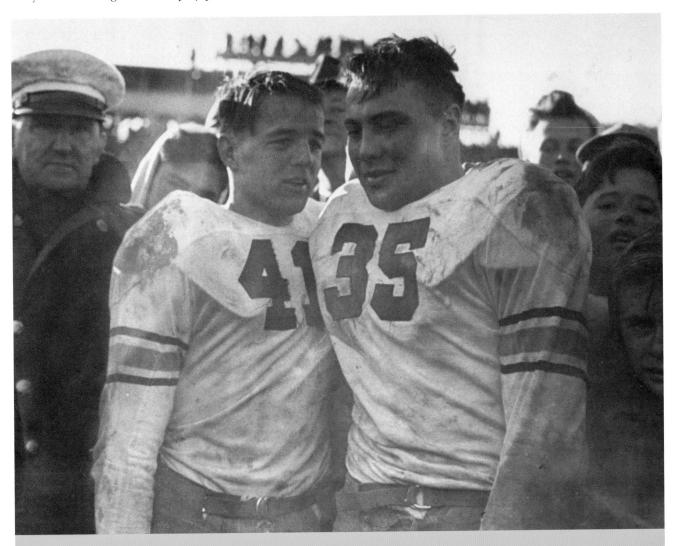

MR. INSIDE AND MR. OUTSIDE: Supporters surround Army teammates Felix "Doc" Blanchard and Glenn Davis, two of the finest college athletes of all time, 1944.

STAT BOX

FIRST GAME

NOVEMBER 29, 1890 • NAVY 24–ARMY 0

LIFETIME HEAD-TO-HEAD RECORD

ARMY 49–NAVY 49 (7 TIES)

MOST COMBINED POINTS

IN ARMY'S 34–30 WIN IN 1998, THE TEAMS SET A SERIES RECORD
FOR COMBINED POINTS

HEISMAN TROPHY WINNERS

ARMY: 3

FELIX BLANCHARD (1945)

GLENN DAVIS (1946)

PETE DAWKINS (1958)

NAVY: 2

JOE BELLINO (1960)

ROGER STAUBACH (1963)

CRITICAL MOMENTS

1944: TO MAKE IT SAFELY TO THE GAME AMID WORLD WAR II DANGERS, THE ARMY'S STUDENTS RODE STEAMSHIPS TO THE GAME, ESCORTED BY NAVY SUBMARINES FOR SAFETY

1963: WITH NAVY LEADING BY 5 POINTS, ARMY COULDN'T GET ITS FINAL PLAY OFF BECAUSE OF THE STADIUM NOISE

1986: NEITHER ARMY NOR NAVY WAS FLAGGED FOR A SINGLE PENALTY, TYING AN ALL-TIME NCAA RECORD

MOST LOPSIDED WIN

NAVY WHOMPED ARMY 51–0 IN 1973

"ROGER THE DODGER": Navy quarterback Roger Staubach with his coach and teammates, 1963. Staubach was possibly Navy's greatest all-time, all-around player.

halfback adept at running the sweep. Together, they led the Cadets to a perfect 9–0 record heading into the big game. Navy was still among the nation's best, ranked No. 2 behind Army. The winner would become the national champion, but beating each other was more important to each school than any mythical title.

With a war on and a plethora of under-used sports arenas from which to choose, President Franklin Roosevelt ordered the game moved to a larger venue, Municipal Stadium in Baltimore, Maryland. Ticket sales went directly to war bonds and more than $60 million was raised. Army won handily 23–7, capturing their first national championship. They repeated the feat the next year, as this time Davis won the Heisman, Army won the game 32–12, and West Point won its second national title.

While Army continued to be a top team after the war,

Navy's fortunes foundered. Thus it was all the sweeter in 1950 when at only 2–6, the Middies walloped the No. 2 ranked Cadets 42–7. A big moment for Army came in 1958, when halfback Pete Dawkins led the Cadets to a 22–6 victory just before being named the winner of the Heisman Trophy.

The 1963 game is among the most memorable, for several reasons. First, the game was postponed for a week after the assassination of President John F. Kennedy. Second, Navy was led by perhaps its greatest all-time, all-around player, quarterback Roger Staubach. The year before, he had led Navy to a win in the big game, passing for two touchdowns, throwing only two incompletions, and leading both teams in rushing. For the 1963 game, "Roger the Dodger" continued his heroics, but Army made it close in the end. Their last-ditch attack placed

THE ETERNAL STRUGGLE: Navy running back Cory Schemm looks downfield while Army's Chad Suitonu gets Schemm in his sights during the 1996 Army–Navy clash.

THROUGHOUT THE LIFE OF THE RIVALRY, THE CONNECTION BETWEEN LIFE ON THE FIELD OF PLAY AND LIFE IN THE FIELD OF WAR HAS BEEN EXPLICIT.

the game firmly among the best ever in the rivalry.

As the game headed toward its end, Army quarterback Rollie Stichweh led his team to within five points, and then back down the field with less than two minutes to go. Knocking on the Navy goal-line

inside the five, Stichweh faced not only the Army 11, but the Middies in the stands, too. Three times he went to the line to call the final, fourth-down-and-goal play, and three times he was forced back by the noise. The officials stopped the clock twice to help Army, but after the third time, the clock made it to 0:00 before Army could get its play off. The game ended as a 21–16 Navy win.

Proving again that there is only one truly desired result in this game, Navy twice in the 1970s chose to go for a game-winning pass instead of an easy tying field goal in the waning moments. Both passes failed, but honor was achieved in trying to win instead of tie. "You only play the Army–Navy game to win," the losing coaches said.

Throughout the life of the rivalry, the connection between life on the field of play and life in the field of war has been explicit. Former players are expected to take the lessons learned on the field, whether against their academy opponents or another foe, and use them in service of their country.

While some of those players take these lessons into many areas of life off the field in business, education, or even life at home, their commanders during their military careers know well how influential time on the gridiron can be.

General Douglas MacArthur famously said about the game, "On the field of friendly strife are sown the seeds that on other fields on other days will bear the fruits of victory."

Not long after he left the presidency, Dwight Eisenhower, a former Army player, wrote to author Gene Schorr about the importance of football.

"I cannot recall a single ex-footballer with whom I came in contact who failed to meet every requirement (of leadership). Personally, I think this was more than coincidental. I believe that football, almost more than any other sport, tends to instill into men the feeling that victory comes through hard—almost slavish—work, team play, self-confidence, and an enthusiasm that amounts to dedication."

The 2004 game brought that connection to mind as forcefully as ever in the series. Following a 42–13 Navy blowout to cap their best season since 1963, Middies players held up three jerseys: those of former teammates and Navy grads Ron Winchester, Scott Zellem, and J. P. Blacksmith. Those three would have been dancing in the stands in celebration.

Instead, they were buried in heroes' graves, killed in action in Iraq.

–J.B.

SPORTS KNOW-IT-ALL

OFFICERS'
PIGSKIN

ARMY

OMAR BRADLEY played lineman for Army in 1914. He became General Omar Bradley, one of the most senior and important leaders of Allied Forces in World War II.

JOE STILLWELL played running back in 1904. During World War II, General "Vinegar Joe" Stillwell led a famous campaign in Burma.

DWIGHT EISENHOWER was a halfback for a short time in 1912. Later, as the more well-known "Ike," he became Supreme Commander of Allied Forces during World War II and later served two terms as president (1951–1960).

NAVY

JONAS INGRAM played fullback and later coached the Midshipmen. In 1914 he was awarded the Congressional Medal of Honor for actions during battles with Mexican forces.

WILLIAM HALSEY was a lineman from 1901 to 1904. In World War II, as Admiral "Bull" Halsey, he led the Pacific fleet to numerous vital victories.

MUHAMMAD ALI *vs.*
JOE FRAZIER

ONE OF THE GREATEST MATCH-UPS OF ALL TIME, ONE THAT IS ALLUDED TO AGAIN AND AGAIN IN THE ANNALS OF sports lore, came out of a total head-to-head time of less than three hours. Less than three hours over three meetings, yet the rivalry between international boxing legend Muhammad Ali and the tough, tenacious, and street-hardened Joe Frazier took on a life of its own, lasting well beyond either of the athlete's careers such that more than thirty years later, memories of their fights are still invoked.

Ali was, by near-consensus, the greatest and most important athlete of the 20th century. ESPN, the Associated Press, and *Sports Illustrated* all named him so in their end-of-the-century top 100 lists. His impact on boxing, on the sports scene, on the greater American culture, and on the world—for much of his working life, no person on the globe was more recognizable—is unquestioned.

Frazier, the man who would become Ali's greatest ring challenge, was his polar opposite in many ways. Though he, like Ali, had earned an Olympic gold medal (Ali in 1960, Frazier four years later), the two men differed entirely in style, approach, attitude, and personality. Yet both were supreme boxers, bringing nearly matched, though dissimilar skills into the ring. Ali was smoothness, grace, and sudden stabbing power. Frazier was determined, bulldog-like attack, with little time or energy for style.

It is the contrasts between the two men, in and out of the ring, combined with the intensity and ferocity of their three legendary bouts, that makes theirs perhaps the greatest individual rivalry in sports history.

THE FIRST FIGHT

By the time of the first Ali–Frazier fight on March 8, 1971, Muhammad Ali had been the white-hot center of the boxing world for nearly a decade, even though for almost three of those years, he had been unable to box. Thanks to his conviction (later overturned) for draft evasion in 1967, Ali had been stripped of his world heavyweight title, famously won from Sonny Liston in 1964. He found himself unable to get a license to box anywhere in the United States, which he could not leave while his case was appealed.

Ali's decision to defy the draft had come as a result of his Muslim faith, to which he had converted in 1964. Changing his name from Cassius Clay to Muhammad Ali (which means "one worthy of praise"), Ali became one of the major symbols of the racially charged atmosphere of the 1960s. Instantly, he changed from photogenic, trash-talking champ to vilified anti-American traitor. "I ain't got no quarrel with no Viet Cong," he said when explaining his decision to not step forward when his name was called.

Ali's conscience-based entry into world politics

ALI WAS, BY NEAR-CONSENSUS, THE GREATEST AND MOST IMPORTANT ATHLETE OF THE 20TH CENTURY.

TALKING SMACK: Muhammad Ali taunts Joe Frazier leading up to their first fight, 1971. Ali went so far as to call Frazier an Uncle Tom.

"I DON'T REMEMBER BREATHING ALL NIGHT LONG": Ali and Frazier exchange blows in their first, highly anticipated fight at Madison Square Garden, 1971.

changed him from sports personality into political personality. It vaulted him beyond the "squared circle" and made him perhaps the first true athlete of the world. His personality, his politics, and his pugilism combined to form a legend. Spouting poetry before fights, bombast afterward, and bringing style and power to the ring in a never-before-seen combination, Ali was, as this fight began, already an international hero.

But he had been away from the ring for most of three years by the time he fought Frazier for the first time. Ali had come back with a couple of warm-up bouts in 1970, after his ongoing court case opened the door to getting his license back. Frazier, meanwhile, had become the champ by beating Jimmy Ellis in 1970 (Ali would not be

fully cleared until the Supreme Court overturned his conviction in June 1971). "Smokin' Joe" could never compete with Ali in the personality category; fans saw only the stolid, workmanlike, yet powerful boxer in the ring and little else. Frazier had never been beaten as a pro, winning 26 bouts with 23 on knockouts.

Ali, too, was undefeated, at 31–0 with 25 knockouts. It was perhaps the first time that two unbeaten fighters faced off for the heavyweight title. The combination of the boxing history and the Ali story made this the "Fight of the Century," by many accounts. To this day, when lists of great boxing matches are held, matches that lived up to their incredible hype, matches that affected the fight game and the sports world in a permanent way, bouts that

STAT BOX

FIRST BOUT: FIGHT OF THE CENTURY

DATE: MARCH 8, 1971

SITE: MADISON SQUARE GARDEN, NEW YORK CITY

TV VIEWERS: APPROX. 300 MILLION

ALI: 215 POUNDS

FRAZIER: 205.5 POUNDS

ODDS: FRAZIER FAVORED 6–5

WINNER: FRAZIER IN A 15-ROUND DECISION

SECOND BOUT: BATTLE OF GIANTS

DATE: JANUARY 28, 1974

SITE: MADISON SQUARE GARDEN, NEW YORK CITY

TV VIEWERS: EXCEEDED 1 BILLION PEOPLE

ALI: 212 POUNDS

FRAZIER: 209 POUNDS

ODDS: ALI FAVORED 8–1

WINNER: ALI IN A 12-ROUND DECISION

THIRD BOUT: THRILLA IN MANILA

DATE: SEPTEMBER 30, 1975

SITE: MANILA, PHILIPPINES

TV VIEWERS: APPROX. 700 MILLION

ALI: 210 POUNDS

FRAZIER: 205 POUNDS

ODDS: ALI FAVORED 2–1

WINNER: ALI IN A 14-ROUND TKO

THE
POETRY
OF ALI

BEFORE A 1963 FIGHT AGAINST DOUG JONES

Jones likes to mix,
So I'll let it go six.
If he talks jive,
I'll cut it to five.
And if he talks some more,
I'll cut it to four.
(Note: Ali won, but it took him ten rounds.)

BEFORE THE EPIC 1964 FIGHT WITH SONNY LISTON

Yes, the crowd did not dream,
When they laid down their money
That they would see
The total eclipse of the Sonny!
I am the greatest!

BEFORE THE 1971 BOUT WITH JOE FRAZIER

I'll be pickin' and pokin'
Pouring water on his smokin'
This might shock and amaze ya
But I'm gonna destroy Joe Frazier!

TAKE THAT!: Ali dances back to avoid a Frazier jab during their first fight, 1971. Despite his pre-fight provoking poetry, Ali lost the match.

ALI ON FILM

ALI (2001)

A slightly fictionalized retelling of the Ali legend from filmmaker Michael Mann. The very popular movie starred rapper-turned-actor Will Smith, who bulked up his slender frame to convincingly portray Ali. Jon Voight turned in a memorable performance as Ali foil Howard Cosell.

WHEN WE WERE KINGS (1996)

This film focuses entirely on the 1974 "Rumble in the Jungle" fight with George Foreman. It was shot at the time, but not released for more than 20 years due to politics in Zaire. The behind-the-scenes access shows another side of Ali, while the public filming demonstrates the immense popularity of the man and the athlete among Africans.

MUHAMMAD ALI, THE GREATEST (1969)

A documentary by William Klein that gathered news clips from two parts of Ali's life—the mid-1960s, when his victories over Liston and conversion to Islam made him famous, and the late 1960s, when his avoidance of the draft made him infamous.

combined mighty personalities with ferocious action, this fight always makes the list, and often at the top.

Ali added his famous poetry to the prefight extravaganza and even visited Frazier at his training camp to verbally attack him, going so far as to call him an Uncle Tom, further inflaming the anti-Ali forces.

The site of the fight was Madison Square Garden, the veritable world capital of big-time boxing. Each fighter was guaranteed $2.5 million for the bout, and more than 300 million people, an enormous audience for the time, were expected to tune in. The Garden itself was packed with more than 20,000 people, seemingly every other one a celebrity. Barbra Streisand and Bill Cosby were among those at ringside. Frank Sinatra himself was taking pictures for *LIFE* magazine. Fifty countries carried the fight live, which was broadcast by announcers in twelve languages. More people ended up watching Ali fight Frazier than had watched Neil Armstrong step onto the moon in 1969, and most did so via paid admission to closed-circuit broadcasts, the "pay-per-view" of the time. It was one of the most played-up, anticipated, headline-making, super-hyped sports events ever.

"I don't remember breathing all night long," wrote Dave Kindred of the *Sporting News* in 1999; the veteran columnist sat second-row ringside in 1971.

Ali charged out, his lightning-fast jab trying to whittle the powerful Frazier down to size. Ali was taunting, teasing, dancing, and ducking from the start, making a show of the fight, trying to get into Frazier's head. It didn't work. By the sixth round, Ali was showing the effects of his long layoff, and Frazier continued to bull ahead, landing hook after hook. Postfight commentators were surprised that Ali had let himself run out of gas so quickly.

Ali hung in there, but Frazier was relentless, at one point in the 11th round making Ali "fold like a carpenter's rule," according to *Sports Illustrated* in a wonderful phrase. Afterward, even Frazier was impressed, however, saying of Ali, "That man can sure take some punches. I went to the country, back home, for some of the shots I hit him with."

SI's Mark Kram said that by the 14th round, both fighters were spent, "like big fish who had wallowed onto a beach," and that Ali's jab had "faded like a sick flower." (Though baseball leads the sports world in literature, boxing can surpass it in poetry.) The man with

MORE PEOPLE ENDED UP WATCHING ALI FIGHT FRAZIER THAN HAD WATCHED NEIL ARMSTRONG STEP ONTO THE MOON.

the best view in the house, the third man in the ring, was as surprised as anyone. "The way they were hitting, I was surprised that it went fifteen," said famed referee Arther Mercante. "They threw some of the best punches I've ever seen."

Though both men had fought bravely, there was one clear winner, and it was not the man loved or hated by "multitudes in every corner of the earth." It was the puncher from Philly, the former farm kid from South Carolina, Smokin' Joe Frazier, who decisively won the Fight of the Century. Every judge had him clearly ahead, with one judge giving him 11 rounds to four for Ali.

Sports Illustrated's cover headline the next week said what many thought at the time: "End of the Ali Legend." But like many others in the sports world, they were wrong.

THE SECOND FIGHT

That the two men would fight again was an inevitability unique to boxing. But by the time it was all arranged, for January 28, 1974, there was nothing on the line except history. Neither fighter was the champ, Frazier having lost his title to George Foreman. Ali, too, had suffered another loss, when Ken Norton had broken his jaw in 1973.

This second bout didn't have nearly the level of anticipation of the first; each fighter got only $1 million (though that was a record for a nontitle fight). The fighters famously started punching and wrestling during a TV interview with Howard Cosell in the week before the fight, but it came off more as show than serious.

In the ring, the action was not nearly as fierce as in the first fight, either. Ali did more grabbing when Frazier powered inside, but his jab also stung Frazier more steadily. An overeager referee, Tony Perez, may have saved Frazier from an early exit. As it was, Ali dominated the fight, and Frazier didn't come out of his corner at the start of the 14th. Round two of the rivalry went to Ali.

This second fight's comparative lethargy and the

record of one win apiece meant that boxing fans could immediately start talking about one thing: a third Ali–Frazier fight, the ultimate rubber match.

For Ali, this second fight was important because it set up his eventual battle for the title against the mighty George Foreman. In that October 1974 fight, the "Rumble in the Jungle" in Zaire, Ali invented a boxing technique and won back his belt. Fans watched in amazement as Ali essentially let the larger Foreman batter him relentlessly for seven rounds. Yet as Ali was back to the ropes with his arms up, the punches were not devastating. "Rope-a-Dope," as Ali's technique came to be called, turned Foreman into a punched-out pussycat while Ali turned into a junkyard dog, knocking out the exhausted champ in the eighth.

YOU AGAIN: Ali and Frazier have a second go, 1974. This time, Ali wins the fight.

THE ULTIMATE RUBBER MATCH: Frazier and Ali battle in their third and final fight, the "Thrilla in Manila," 1975. Ali won only by surviving longer.

The championship was once more Ali's. He became the first man in heavyweight boxing to twice regain a crown; it's no small matter that Ali had lost that crown in the Madison Square Garden fight against Frazier. Now the pressure was even stronger to defend it, and so Ali turned back to his archrival for one more epic match.

THE THIRD FIGHT

Few sports events have been as poetically or memorably named as the "Thrilla in Manila," the third Ali–Frazier duel in 1975. This time Ali was defending the heavyweight title that he had won from Foreman, and Frazier was the challenger. The world was all on Ali's side, his image and reputation having been softened by time, victory, and his own indomitable personality. It helped, of course, that most of the United States had come over to his side and point of view on the Vietnam War, which had ignominiously ended not long before with the fall of Saigon.

Ali's popularity around the world had continued to

rise as well, and after the success of the Foreman fight in Zaire, promoters looked elsewhere on the globe for a fight that was nearly as anticipated as their first encounter. They settled on Manila, in the Philippines. Ali certainly liked the rhyme scheme the city site provide him, boasting that it would be a "killa and a thrilla and a chilla when I get the gorilla in Manila."

More than 700 million people were in the estimated TV audience, and they were treated to a display of courage and ferocity the likes of which boxing has never seen since. It was truly epic, it was Homerian, it was stupefying. That two men could stand such punishment, and more amazingly, return for more, shocked the audience. It was brutal, animal, emotional—all in the fierce tropical heat. Back and forth, blow for blow, the two men staged a battle of bravery.

"Old Joe Frazier, I thought you was washed up," Ali was heard to say.

"Somebody told you all wrong, pretty boy," Frazier mumbled back.

The fight ebbed and flowed like mighty waves on a beach. Ali easily won the first half of the fight, but Frazier found something deep inside himself that let him battle back to control in the middle rounds. Then Ali returned, his jab finding home again and again on Frazier's battered head.

Nearly blinded by swelling, Frazier did not leave his corner to start the 15th round. "No man will ever forget what you did here today," said his merciful trainer Eddie Futch, as he held his man back from the ring.

In the end, Ali had simply survived longer.

"It was like death," he said afterward. "Closest thing to dyin' that I know of."

It left, in the words of Mark Kram, "millions limp." Though both men fought on, Frazier until 1976 (with one inconsequential comeback fight in 1981) and Ali, amazingly, until 1981, their records and boxing lives essentially ended on that steamy night in Manila. While they started their storied rivalry with the Fight of the Century, they ended with an Epic for the Ages. Boxing is a hard sport, a sport seemingly out of another, darker time. But ever since it moved from brawl to big-time in the late 1800s, it has been the last refuge of courage in sports. And no two men showed it more than Ali and Frazier in Manila.

—J.B.

SPORTS KNOW-IT-ALL

AFTER THE RING

ALI

• Suffering from Parkinson's Syndrome, Ali has nonetheless continued in his role as worldwide ambassador.

• Travels frequently, promoting his faith and supporting a variety of national and international charities, especially those relating to Africa and medical relief.

• In 1990, helped secure the release of prisoners taken in Iraq before start of Gulf War.

• In 1996, lit torch to open Summer Olympics in Atlanta.

• Named U.N. Ambassador of Peace in 2000 by U.N. Secretary-General Kofi Annan.

• Author of 2004 book *The Soul of a Butterfly: Reflections on Life's Journey*.

• Opened Muhammad Ali Center in Louisville, Kentucky in 2005, a cultural and education center.

FRAZIER

• Briefly tried a singing and nightclub career.

• Owns a gym in Philadelphia.

• Attends boxing dinners and special events, and remains a popular figure in boxing world.

OHIO STATE *vs.* MICHIGAN

COLLEGE FOOTBALL FANS REMAIN LOYAL FIRST TO THEIR OWN SCHOOLS; THEY ROOT MOST LOUDLY AND EMOTE MOST deeply for dear old alma mater U. But as they look around the landscape, there are very few of those true fans, fans who truly care about the wider game, who have seen what the games can mean to schools and the nation . . . very few indeed who can dispute that University of Michigan vs. Ohio State University is the greatest college football rivalry ever. Or should we say Ohio State vs. Michigan?

In 2003 the teams played the 100th game of this historic rivalry, a match-up that has roots dating back to 1897. In that century-plus of football, the games have turned the tide of the national championship race numerous times. Dozens and dozens of future NFL stars have worn the maize and blue of Michigan or the crimson and silver of Ohio State. From the first moment of each season until the final whistle of the last game (and their head-to-head battle has been the last regular-season game for each school since 1935), every player, coach, student, and professor has only one thought: Beat _____ (insert other school's name here).

When the rivalry began, the two schools actually were just continuing an intrastate rivalry dating back to the 1830s, when both places claimed Toledo as part of their new territory. It took the efforts of future president Andrew Jackson to soothe the angry parties: Michigan got to become a state, Ohio got Toledo (no comment on who got the better deal). But it started a Midwestern Melee that is reenacted each year. (In 2004 Ohio banned the import of wood from Michigan over some insect fears. No objections were raised by any affected Ohians: This was Michigan, after all.) By 1897, when the football teams first met, Michigan was a football veteran, playing its 17th season; OSU was a relative babe in the grass, having played only seven seasons, and those on a far lower level than the Wolverines.

However, Ohio State probably deserves the most credit for keeping the game going in its early years; they got kicked up and down the field on a regular basis, but kept coming back. Michigan was the finest college team in the land for most of the first decade of the 20th century; Ohio State was just trying to stay alive. Michigan won the opener 34–0, and, though OSU forged a remarkable scoreless tie in the next meeting in 1900, the Wolverines won 12 of the next 13 games (their 1902 win by 86–0 is still a record for the series). Not until 1919–1921 did OSU win more than one in a row. But then Michigan reeled off another streak, this time of six straight. Since then, no team has dominated for more than four straight, and they've generally alternated wins or short streaks.

In 1922, in part thanks to the growing popularity of the rivalry, OSU opened its huge new Ohio Stadium; of course, in the dedication game, Michigan came in and

> IN A CENTURY-PLUS OF FOOTBALL, THE GAMES HAVE TURNED THE TIDE OF THE NATIONAL CHAMPIONSHIP RACE NUMEROUS TIMES.

"OLD 98": Michigan's Heisman-winning Tom Harmon tears up the field, 1939. The following year, he would contribute mightily to Michigan's demolishing OSU.

HOPALONG HEADS UPFIELD: OSU's Heisman-winning "Hopalong" Cassidy works his magic, 1955.

spoiled the party, winning 19–0. In 1927 Michigan opened its stadium, which would eventually see more than 100,000 fans at every annual rivalry game; OSU couldn't play the spoiler, too, falling 21–0.

The 1940s featured two of the best players to have taken part in the series. In 1940 Tom Harmon of Michigan, "Old 98," for his uniform number, tore up the Big Ten. He capped off his Heisman-Trophy-winning season

by running for three touchdowns, passing for two others, and adding four extra-point kicks in the Wolverines' 40–0 shellacking of OSU. Four years later, it was Ohio State's turn to win the game and take home the Heisman. Running back Les Horvath scored the go-ahead touchdown in the Buckeyes' 18–14 win and then was named the nation's top college player.

The game in 1950 remains one of the most famous

GOLDEN
PANTS

Through the years, Ohio State players have taken home sacks full of awards: Heisman Trophies, Lombardi Awards, Thorpe Awards, All-America honors, places of honor in the College Football Hall of Fame. But most of the award-winners will tell you that their most prized trophies (if they earned one) are small enough to hang from a necklace—a tiny pair of gold football pants.

The pants, designed as a sort of charm as on a bracelet or, in the old days, on a watch chain, are awarded to every player in every Ohio State victory over hated Michigan. The tradition started in 1934 thanks to coach Francis Schmidt. He led his team to a 34–0 trashing of the Wolverines that year, the school's biggest victory yet in the series. Earlier in the season, he had told his players not to fear Michigan, "because they put their pants on one leg at a time, same as everybody else." Boosters of the team remembered the quote after the trouncing and created the now-unmistakable and very unique award.

in the series, not for what it meant on a national scale, but for what the players—and fans—went through. The week of the game, the Columbus, Ohio, area was hit by the worst blizzard in four decades; five inches of snow were on the ground and more fell throughout the game. The wind whipped around at nearly 30 miles per hour. Had the contest not been needed to decide the conference title, it might not have been played. As it was, some 50,000 people braved the elements to watch a punting contest. Unable to run, catch, or pass, the teams essentially took turns punting the ball back and forth. A field goal, an amazing feat in the face of the blowing wind, by OSU legend Vic Janowicz gave them a lead. Michigan scored on a safety after a blocked kick. Another blocked punt was recovered by the Wolverines for what proved to be the winning score in a 9–3 win. "It was terrible," Janowicz said afterward. "My hands were numb. I had no feeling in them. You knew what you wanted to do, you just couldn't do it."

Ohio coach Woody Hayes (see box on page 56) took over in the 1951 season and was soon whipping the rivalry up even further. His intense hatred of Michigan colored his every move. In his first 18 years leading Ohio State, the Wolverines won only one Big Ten title (in 1964) and in Hayes' eyes, that was one too many.

Though the teams split the rivalry games in the 1950s, Ohio State enjoyed the most overall success, winning national titles in 1954 and 1957. In 1955 OSU's Howard "Hopalong" Cassidy capped off his own Heisman season with 146 yards and a touchdown in his team's 17–0 shutout.

Heading into the 1968 game, Hayes had built his finest team yet. A powerful defense and a balanced offense proved to be just too much for every team they faced, including Michigan. Ahead by only seven at halftime, OSU whomped through the second half with ease, finally putting a 50–14 spanking on Michigan. After a Rose Bowl win over USC, OSU earned its first national title in 11 years.

The next year, however, in came Bo (see box on page 56). Under new coach and former Ohio State assistant Bo Schembechler, Michigan stood in the way of Ohio State's second straight national title. Schembechler's name forever became mud in Ohio for his traitorous move to the enemy. In a game he called the worst defeat of his life, Hayes lost to 17-point underdog Michigan 24–12.

LET IT SNOW: Ohio and Michigan players scramble for the ball in the coldest game in memory, as 50,000 sturdy Midwestern fans look on, 1950.

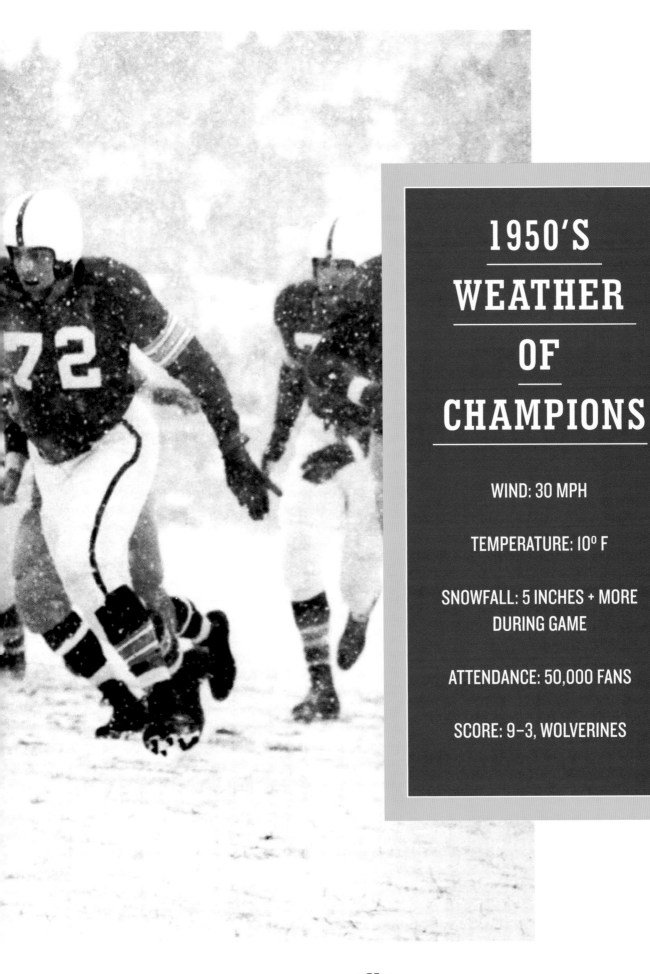

1950'S
WEATHER
OF
CHAMPIONS

WIND: 30 MPH

TEMPERATURE: 10° F

SNOWFALL: 5 INCHES + MORE
DURING GAME

ATTENDANCE: 50,000 FANS

SCORE: 9–3, WOLVERINES

HIGHLIGHT REEL

★ ★ ★ ★ ★

Woody vs. Bo

Neither played a down in the games. Neither scored a touchdown or kicked a field goal. But together Ohio State coach Woody Hayes and Michigan coach Bo Schembechler racheted up the schools' rivalry to a fever pitch not seen before or since, in what is known as the Ten Year War. Here are some highlights:

1968- Thrashing the Wolverines 50–14 in a game that would help the Buckeyes win the national championship, Hayes ordered his team to go for two after scoring their sixth touchdown. In one of college football's most famous postgame quotes, he said, when asked why he'd gone for two then (a very unsportsmanlike move outside the context of such a rivalry), "Because they wouldn't let us go for three." Hayes would not fill his gas tank in the state of Michigan. He would not let his players sleep overnight there before the game, once bunking in nearby Toledo and busing in on game day. Though Michigan was rife with great schoolboy talent, Hayes nearly always refused to recruit his players from there. His entire coaching life, year-round, was aimed at defeating Michigan.

1969- Bo Schembechler, one of Hayes' trusted assistants, turned traitor and took the Michigan head coaching job. The betrayal was made worse when Schembechler used his deep knowledge of Hayes to guide Michigan to a stunning 24–12 upset of an Ohio State team then ranked No. 1 in the nation. To his dying day, Hayes called it the worst defeat of his life.

1973- OSU was No. 1 and Michigan No. 4 at kickoff. Missed field goals by the Michigan kicker kept the game an unsatisfying 10–10 tie. Michigan felt it was a big win and that they'd be chosen to go to the Rose Bowl (the teams having tied in the conference standings, a committee would select one to travel to Pasadena). But wily old Hayes was way ahead of them, and he made his influence felt, allegedly contacting conference officials to express his opinion . . . and Ohio State went west.

Bo and Woody looked across 53 $\frac{1}{2}$ yards of grass ten times. Eight of those games decided the conference title; each school headed to Pasadena five times. The final total was five for OSU, four for Michigan, and one tie.

AT PEACE: Ohio State running back Archie Griffin poses with his Heisman Trophy, 1975. Griffin remains the only two-time Heisman Trophy winner.

OHIO COACH WOODY HAYES TOOK OVER IN THE 1951 SEASON . . . HIS INTENSE HATRED OF MICHIGAN COLORED HIS EVERY MOVE.

The two men would lead their squads against each other for a decade and every time they met, it was as near a war as football can be. Hayes dominated from 1973–1975, helped in part by running back Archie Griffin, the only two-time Heisman Trophy winner ever. Michigan then won four of five games from 1976–1980, though OSU's 1979 win in that period was an 18–15 classic nail-biter.

The years leading up to the end of the millennium were tough ones for Buckeye fans. From 1985 to 2000, their heroes won only three of the rivalry games. Coach John Cooper was the symbol of this sad era. In his 13 years leading the Buckeyes, his winning percentage was north of .700, an impressive record for a coach, but in all that time, he managed to beat Michigan only twice.

STAT BOX

FIRST GAME

OCTOBER 16, 1897 • MICHIGAN 34–OHIO STATE 0

LIFETIME HEAD-TO-HEAD RECORD

MICHIGAN 57–OHIO 38 (6 TIES)

NATIONAL CHAMPIONSHIPS

OHIO STATE: 5

1942, 1954, 1957, 1968, 2002

MICHIGAN: 6

1901, 1902, 1932, 1947, 1948, 1997

HEISMAN TROPHY WINNERS

OHIO STATE: 5

LES HORVATH (1944) , VIC JANO-WICZ (1950), HOWARD CASSADY (1955), ARCHIE GRIFFIN (1974, 1975), EDDIE GEORGE (1995)

MICHIGAN: 3

TOM HARMON (1940), DESMOND HOWARD (1991), CHARLES WOODSON (1997)

PLAYERS WHO MADE PRO HALL OF FAME

OHIO STATE: 6

SID GILLMAN, COACH

LOU GROZA, TACKLE/KICKER

DANTE LAVELLI, END

JIM PARKER, GUARD/TACKLE

PAUL WARFIELD, WIDE RECEIVER

BILL WILLIS, GUARD

MICHIGAN: 7

GEORGE ALLEN, COACH

DAN DIERDORF, TACKLE

LEN FORD, END

BENNY FRIEDMAN, QUARTERBACK

BILL HEWITT, END

ELROY HIRSCH, HALFBACK/END

TOM MACK, GUARD

I'LL TAKE THAT: Ohio's Michael Doss intercepts a pass meant for Michigan wide receiver Marquise Walker in the schools' 2001 competition. The Buckeyes won, 26–20.

He also watched his team's undefeated record and national championship hopes disappear into a sea of maize and blue on three different occasions. One such heartache came in 1996, when No. 2–ranked Ohio State dominated the game until a late touchdown got Michigan back into it and a late field goal gave them an improbable 13–9 win.

In 1997 OSU watched in pain as Michigan rode a 20–14 victory in the rivalry game into a postseason Rose Bowl win to earn its first national championship since 1968. Michigan also boasted a pair of Heisman winners in this era: wide receiver/kick returner Desmond Howard in 1991 and defensive back Charles Woodson in 1997.

By 2001, Cooper was gone, due in large part to his inability to beat Michigan.

The years since have been a bit better, with OSU coming out on top three of the past four years, including their national championship season in 2002 (though even then, the game came down to a final-play, end-zone interception by OSU to seal their victory).

But no matter what the records, when these two schools butt heads, it is a game that is truly the finest example of college sports rivalry in the land. It's got tradition, emotion, stars, national import, and two great fight songs. What more do you need?

—J.B.

DUKE vs. UNC

I N THE MOMENTS IMMEDIATELY FOLLOWING THE UNIVERSITY OF NORTH CAROLINA'S 75–70 WIN OVER ILLINOIS IN THE 2005
NCAA national championship basketball game, Tar Heel fans had every reason to be happy, proud, boastful even. And so as fans filed out of the Edward Jones Dome in St. Louis that night, their thoughts inevitably turned toward Tobacco Road back home in Carolina, but not just to the giddy revelers on Chapel Hill's Franklin Street who were lighting up the night with bonfires. Instead, as is so often the case, those Tar Heel fans couldn't help but think of the next town over from Chapel Hill: Durham (or, as a Chapel Hillian might put it, "Derm, as in germ"). The thought of Duke University fans being as miserable as North Carolina fans were ecstatic warmed the heart of nearly every Tar Heel backer, and a cry soon went up from young students to elderly boosters alike—"Duke sucks! Duke sucks!"

Of course, as with all things in this long rivalry of one-upsmanship, this was merely delayed payback for Duke fans, who, in the waning seconds of their own national championship win in 2001 (and, in fact, during most games, period) struck up their customary "Go to hell, Carolina!" chant.

To question such acts as juvenile will only guarantee a misunderstanding of one of college sports' most passionate rivalries, one that is great both because of its local fervor and national appeal. Duke University, a private school, and the University of North Carolina, a public school, are separated by just eight miles of highway on United States 15-501, yet each meeting between their perennially top-quality basketball teams is always the biggest sports event of the day or even the week. Both are academic institutions of high distinction, and yet the intensity of feeling engendered by each school's storied basketball team colors general feelings toward the respective universities (different shades of blue, of course). When UNC, the first public university in the United States, was celebrating its bicentennial in October 1993, longtime newsman and UNC alum Charles Kuralt received his biggest cheers for this line: "I speak for all of us who could not afford to go to Duke. And would not have even if we could have afforded it."

The differences between the two universities are well-noted. Duke is small, its student body is drawn mostly from the northeast, and it revels in its distinction as the "Harvard of the South." Its campus, full of Gothic architecture and stone buildings, is a far cry from the brick walkways and tree-filled quads of UNC. And while Durham is a city, Chapel Hill was once named the "best college town" in America by *Sports Illustrated*. UNC is home to 24,000 students, of whom 82 percent must, by state law, come from North Carolina.

Certainly, there has been plenty for fans of each school to root for. Like the Lancastrians and the Yorkists, each

A CRY SOON WENT UP FROM YOUNG STUDENTS TO ELDERLY BOOSTERS ALIKE—"DUKE SUCKS! DUKE SUCKS!"

DE-FENSE!: Duke's Sheldon Williams (#23) blocks a shot by UNC's Marvin Williams (#24) in March 2005. The Duke defense wasn't quite strong enough; UNC won 75–73.

COACH VS. COACH

The quickest way to start an argument between a Duke and North Carolina fan is to ask who is the better coach—Dean Smith or Mike Krzyzewski? Their loyal fans might not acknowledge it, but the two coaches are actually quite similar. Each is from the Midwest (Smith from Kansas, Krzyzewski from Chicago), each coached at a service academy (Smith was an assistant at Air Force in the 1950s, Coach K was the head man at Army from 1976–1980), each had to endure repeated calls for their firing until winning an ACC title in their sixth seasons, and each ultimately survived by beating their rival school.

In January 1965, fourth-year head-man Smith and the Tar Heels returned from a loss at Wake Forest to find an effigy of the 33-year-old coach hanging high. Using the slight as motivation, North Carolina went to Durham and beat No. 8 Duke in its next game. It was the turning point in Smith's career.

Nearly 20 years later, firmly entrenched as the premier program in college basketball, Smith and his No. 1–ranked Tar Heels entered Durham to face an unranked Duke team led by a young coach in his fourth season in the ACC trying to keep his job. Though Carolina won 78–73, Krzyzewski stood up to what he called a "double-standard" in the ACC: Carolina and everyone else. Coach K and Duke were starting to defeat other ACC teams, which was all well and good. However, doing well against Carolina—winning, or at least not getting shown up should you lose—is the key to success for any Duke coach. Before the season was over, Krzyzewski signed a five-year contract extension and two years later had his first Final Four team.

Eventually, both men would wind up in the Hall of Fame with a roll call of accomplishments that could stretch from Durham to Chapel Hill:

COACH SMITH

Retired in 1997 after 36 years
879 wins
17 ACC regular-season titles
13 ACC Tournament titles
11 Final Fours
2 national championships

COACH KRZYZEWSKI

At Duke since 1981
721 wins
10 ACC regular-season titles
9 ACC Tournament titles
10 Final Fours
3 national championships

On this point, there can be no debate: both are among the greatest coaches of all time.

TWO LEGENDS: UNC coach Dean Smith (left) cuts the net after his team wins the NCAA title, 1993. Duke coach Mike Krzyzewski (right) does likewise after his team captures the ACC Tournament title in 2001.

has a claim to the throne as king of college basketball. Not only do the players graduate and the programs operate without a hint of NCAA scandal, but they succeed like no teams in the country. North Carolina's 1,860 wins are the second-most all-time in Division I. Duke is fourth on that list with 1,764 victories. In 52 seasons of ACC basketball, one of the two schools has won a regular-season or tournament title a mind-boggling 45 times (17 regular-season and 15 tourney titles for the Blue Devils, 24 regular season and 15 tournament titles for the Tar Heels). Duke has had 31 All-America players, including such luminaries as Art Heyman, Johnny Dawkins, Christian Laettner, Bobby Hurley, Grant Hill, Shane Battier, and Jason Williams. Among North Carolina's 39 All-Americas are Billy Cunningham, Phil Ford, James Worthy, Michael Jordan, Jerry Stackhouse, Antawn Jamison, and Vince Carter. The Tar Heels have been to 16 Final Fours, more than any other school, and won five NCAA tournaments. Duke

has advanced to 14 Final Fours, winning three titles. Each has employed a coach of legendary stature, Dean Smith (who holds an NCAA men's record of 879 wins) from 1961–1997 at Carolina and Mike Krzyzewski (ten Final Fours), who just completed his 25th year at Duke.

That kind of success can cause both pressure and motivation to keep up. In 1993, after Duke became the first team since the UCLA dynasty of the 1960s and 1970s to win back-to-back NCAA titles, Tar Heel forward George Lynch admitted that part of his team's motivation was to shut up talk about the Blue Devils, which Carolina did by winning the national championship.

Such "anything-you-can-do-I-can-do-better" attitude has existed virtually since January 24, 1920, when North Carolina beat Duke 36–25 in the teams' first meeting ever. In the 85 years since, the Tar Heels have built a 124–95 advantage in the series, though lately the teams have taken turns owning the other. Between March 1993

BLUE ON BLUE: Duke's Elton Brand (#42) tries to guard UNC's Brendan Haywood (#00), 1999. This time, the Duke defense had its game on, and they defeated UNC 89–77.

and March 1998, the Tar Heels won 10 of 12 games, including the most-hyped contest in the series' history, which came on February 5, 1998. No. 1 Duke strode into the Dean E. Smith Center in Chapel Hill to take on No. 2 UNC and left the victims of a 97–73 evisceration that Tar Heel fans remember fondly as the Double Blowout Game (no sooner had UNC's 16-point halftime lead been cut to four than the Tar Heels outscored Duke 24–4 to close out the game).

Duke responded by winning 14 of the next 17 match-up games through the end of the 2005 season, often by embarrassingly wide margins. The low point for Carolina came in 2001–02, with the Tar Heels suffering through a school-worst 8–20 nightmare of a season. Duke stomped the Heels so completely during the regular season (average margin of victory: 27 points) that North Carolina head coach Matt Doherty conceded his team could no longer compete straight up with Duke. He ordered his team to hold the ball during their ACC Tournament quarterfinal match-up with the Blue Devils in a vain attempt to remain competitive. The tactic worked for

a time, but Duke won 90–76, the second time in four years they had won three games from the Tar Heels in a single season.

As Duke evolved into the model college basketball program, North Carolina, like the rest of the nation, struggled to catch up. The irony—delicious to Duke fans, painful to Carolina fans—was that the reverse had been true for so long. Carolina earned its place as the "IBM of college basketball" by winning at least 20 games for 31 consecutive years between 1971 and 2001 and going to a record 27 straight NCAA Tournaments from 1975–2001. But by the early 1990s, it was clear that the tectonic plates of power had shifted in central North Carolina. Duke was now king, going to an incredible seven Final Fours in nine years between 1986 and 1994. Then, after a brief dip in the mid-90s, they became the first team to finish four straight seasons ranked No. 1 in the country (1999, 2000, 2001, 2002).

"You know what I really like?" Krzyzewski was quoted as saying of UNC in *Sports Illustrated* in 1995. "We know they're doing it right, and they know we're doing it

STAT BOX

FIRST GAME

JANUARY 24, 1920 • DUKE 19–UNC 18

LIFETIME HEAD-TO-HEAD RECORD

UNC 124–DUKE 95

FINAL FOUR ATTENDANCES

DUKE: 14

1963, 1964, 1966, 1978, 1986,
1988, 1989, 1990, 1991, 1992,
1994, 1999, 2001, 2004

UNC: 16

1924, 1946, 1957, 1967, 1968, 1969,
1972, 1977, 1981, 1982, 1993, 1995,
1997, 1998, 2000, 2005

NATIONAL CHAMPIONSHIPS

DUKE: 3

1991, 1992, 2001

UNC: 5

1924, 1957, 1982, 1993, 2005

NATIONAL PLAYERS OF THE YEAR

DUKE

DICK GROAT, 1952

ART HEYMAN, 1963

JOHNNY DAWKINS, 1986

DANNY FERRY, 1989

CHRISTIAN LAETTNER, 1992

ELTON BRAND, 1999

SHANE BATTIER, 2001

JASON WILLIAMS, 2001, 2002

J. J. REDICK, 2005

UNC

JACK COBB, 1926

GEORGE GLAMACK, 1940, 1941

LENNIE ROSENBLUTH, 1957

PHIL FORD, 1978

JAMES WORTHY, 1982

MICHAEL JORDAN, 1983, 1984

KENNY SMITH, 1987

ANTAWN JAMISON, 1998

right. They have their style of doing things, and we have ours. But it's all good. Not just good, it's excellent. And in an environment of excellence, we've made each other better."

Don't mistake those words for a sign of détente. Indeed, the Duke–Carolina rivalry is fueled by equal parts success and passion, which has been known to boil over. In 1961 a brawl requiring ten police officers to break up erupted between the players when Larry Brown (yes, the same Brown who became a long-running NBA coach) of UNC and Art Heyman of Duke squared off underneath the basket in one of the worst fights in ACC history. Twenty-eight years later, in the finals of the ACC Tournament, the two teams again did battle, in more ways than one, as Carolina won a rugged final 77–74 that featured nearly as many bodies hitting the floor as shots finding the net. Finally, in the 2003 regular-season finale, North Carolina head coach Matt Doherty got into a shouting match with Duke assistant coach Chris Collins on the court during a time-out. It nearly escalated into a brawl when Duke reserve Andre Buckner shoved Doherty in the chest. Yet beginning with that game—an 82–79 Carolina win—the teams' next five regular-season meetings (three wins for Duke, two for UNC) have been decided by a total of 13 points.

Those kinds of classic match-ups are the rule, not the exception, whenever Duke and Carolina line up across from one another. There was the famous 1974 game in Chapel Hill when North Carolina rallied from eight points down with 17 seconds left to force overtime on a 35-foot shot from Walter Davis (there were no three-pointers in college basketball at the time). Carolina went on to win 96–92. In 1981 Duke's Gene Banks began his Senior Day (when graduating seniors are honored before the home fans) by throwing roses to the crowd at Cameron Indoor Stadium, then nailed a turnaround jump shot at the buzzer to force overtime in a game Duke went on to win 66–65. "It's the closest I've ever felt to God, and I don't mean that to be blasphemous," Banks has since said.

Indeed, a win against the archrival has often left fans feeling heavenly. Yet such is the state of mutual respect that nearly all agree the one game that best symbolizes the rivalry was one in which both teams shone. It was played in the sultry confines of Duke's Cameron Indoor Stadium on February 2, 1995. A mighty North Carolina team, destined for the Final Four, ranked No. 2 in the nation and led by All-Americas Jerry Stackhouse and Rasheed Wallace, tipped off against an undermanned Duke team that staggered into the game at 0–7 in the ACC, missing not only its requisite level of talent, but also head coach Mike Krzyzewski, out for the season with a bad back and exhaustion.

Carolina jumped to a 17-point first half lead, helped by Stackhouse's memorable reverse jam, but Duke rallied to go ahead by 12 in the second half. This time, Carolina recovered to force overtime and seemed to have the game won when it went ahead by eight with just 20 seconds to play. But Duke chopped the deficit to three and had Carolina's Serge Zwikker on the free throw line with four seconds left. Zwikker missed both and Duke's Jeff Capel furiously pushed the ball up the floor. He released the ball just before the clock hit triple zeroes. When it crashed through the net, the biggest roar ever heard in the old building went up. That Carolina went on to win 102–100 in the second overtime—surviving two Duke shots at the buzzer—was almost anticlimactic. For in that evening, Duke and North Carolina had proven that their rivalry transcends records, coaches, players, fans, universities, or locations alone. It is all of those things and it is bigger than all of those things. It is why at the conclusion of every game these two titans play, someone, player or coach, will inevitably be asked how a game between these two could possibly have been so good . . . again. And that person will shake his head and offer the only explanation necessary. "Because it's Duke and Carolina."

"IN AN ENVIRONMENT OF EXCELLENCE, WE'VE MADE EACH OTHER BETTER" —COACH KRZYZEWSKI

—TED KEITH

Ted Keith is a writer and reporter for *Sports Illustrated for Kids.*

MAKING EACH OTHER BETTER: UNC's Jackie Manuel and Duke's Sheldon Williams battle midair for the ball, 2005. Coach K believes the teams' respective excellence improves both performances.

ALABAMA vs. AUBURN

I T MAY SURPRISE FANS IN RED SOX NATION AND BOOSTERS OF THE BRONX BOMBERS TO LEARN, BUT THERE MAY BE NO more passionate rivalry in all of sports than University of Alabama–Auburn University in college football. Within Alabama's borders, where football is king and there are no professional teams to compete for the attention of its fans, both schools have a devoted, year-round following that is consumed by the game with an almost religious fervor. The University of Alabama is in Tuscaloosa, and its archrival is about 200 miles away in Auburn. There are few people in the state who are not committed to one school or the other in the annual Iron Bowl, so named because Birmingham, the traditional site of the game, sits atop huge deposits of iron ore. The Iron Bowl

Four hundred fifty people were at Birmingham's Lakeview Baseball Park on February 22, 1893, to witness an Auburn victory in the first game of what is now the nation's most spiteful intrastate college rivalry. More than a century after that first meeting, the game is still the state's great divider. The outcome of an Alabama–Auburn match-up has been known to wreck families, ruin friendships, sour business deals, and stir political debate among the state's legislators. The teams have played 69 times (through 2004) with Alabama holding an eight-game edge in the series.

John Heisman, the pioneering coach for whom col-

WHILE THERE ARE OTHER FIERCE, INTRASTATE COLLEGE FOOTBALL RIVALRIES, THE IRON BOWL ALMOST LITERALLY BRINGS AN ENTIRE STATE TO A STANDSTILL.

until recently had been held every year at a neutral site, Legion Field, with tickets distributed evenly between the schools, fueling the electricity of a heated college gridiron battle that is played only once a year; a single contest for bragging rights that last 364 days.

While there are other fierce, intrastate college football rivalries—Texas–Texas A&M, Georgia–Georgia Tech, USC–UCLA, and Florida–Florida State, to name a few—the Iron Bowl almost literally brings an entire state to a standstill. And they've been standing there for more than 100 years (though there was a Hatfield-McCoy–like split that kept the game from being played for more than 40 years!).

lege football's top honor is named, started his coaching career at Auburn in 1895 by routing Alabama, 48–0, in Tuscaloosa. The Auburn Tigers were the early dominators, winning seven of the first 11 meetings between the schools. The 1907 game ended in a 6–all tie due to the gritty play of Alabama's defense, which earned the team its famous nickname; after the game, which was played in a sea of red mud, a newspaper writer for the *Birmingham Age-Herald* dubbed Alabama the "Crimson Tide."

After that stalemate the series was suspended because of an argument between the schools over officiating. Auburn wanted an impartial referee from the North to

PERFECT FORM: Auburn's Jaret Holmes kicks the winning 39-yard field goal against Alabama, 1997.

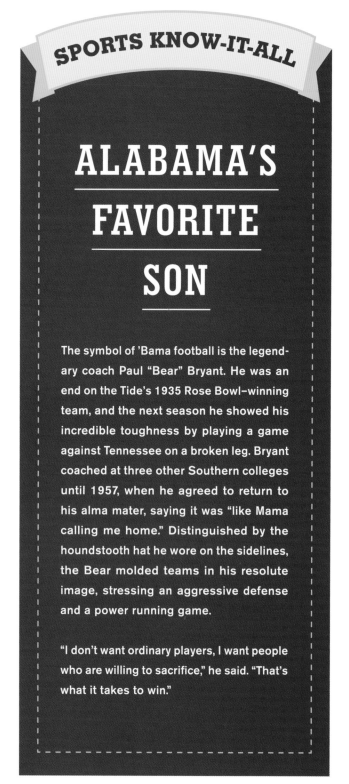

ALABAMA'S FAVORITE SON

The symbol of 'Bama football is the legendary coach Paul "Bear" Bryant. He was an end on the Tide's 1935 Rose Bowl–winning team, and the next season he showed his incredible toughness by playing a game against Tennessee on a broken leg. Bryant coached at three other Southern colleges until 1957, when he agreed to return to his alma mater, saying it was "like Mama calling me home." Distinguished by the houndstooth hat he wore on the sidelines, the Bear molded teams in his resolute image, stressing an aggressive defense and a power running game.

"I don't want ordinary players, I want people who are willing to sacrifice," he said. "That's what it takes to win."

resumed, an intensity that has not relented. Several cities, including Montgomery and Mobile, were considered as hosts for the game, but Birmingham was chosen because it had the largest stadium in the state, the 44,000-seat Legion Field. The dispute officially ended at a "Bury the Hatchet" ceremony before the game, which 'Bama won in a laugher, 55–0. Alabama was favored the next year too, but the upset-minded Tigers shocked the Tide, 14–13, and one of the nation's preeminent football rivalries was officially reborn.

Like the Boston–New York rivalry in baseball, the two Alabama schools have distinct personalities. 'Bama has captured nine national championships in its illustrious football history, and the team's fans have adopted an air of smug superiority. The Crimson Tide has more than 50 bowl game appearances and more than 30 bowl wins, both of which are the most of any team in NCAA history. The Tide has won a record 21 Southeastern Conference titles. Auburn fans, by contrast, carry a chip on their shoulder caused by playing second fiddle for so long and can come across like underappreciated stepchildren.

When Alabama blanked Auburn in 1959 for its first win over the Tigers in five years, the Tide had definitely turned. Alabama ruled college football during the 1960s, winning three national championships in five years. Even away from the football field, famed Alabama coach Paul "Bear" Bryant was the state's favorite native son; he received one-and-a-half votes for the Presidential nomination from the Alabama delegation at the Democratic convention in Chicago in 1968.

TOUGH BEAR: A young Joe Namath confers with Alabama coach Paul "Bear" Bryant, 1964.

work future games; Alabama wanted a Southerner. The schools could not come to terms on the issue for 41 years. Finally, in the spring of 1948, the two university presidents decided the feud had gone on long enough and agreed the series should resume using officials from both above and below the Mason-Dixon Line.

The fact that the two schools stopped playing for decades only added to the intensity of the series when it

In 1971 both schools entered the Iron Bowl with undefeated records for the first time, in a match-up broadcast on national television. Heisman Trophy–winning quarterback Pat Sullivan led Auburn, but the hard-charging halfback Johnny Musso carried Alabama to a hard-earned victory. But perhaps the most famous, and easily the most talked about, game between the two schools was the December 2, 1972, contest at Legion Field. A few days before the game, Coach Bear Bryant incited an uproar when he told reporters: "Sure I'd like to beat Notre Dame, don't get me wrong. But nothing matters more than beating that cow college on the other side of the state. I'd rather beat [Auburn] once than beat Texas ten times."

That set the stage for a performance that Crimson Tide fans would like to forget. Undefeated and second-ranked Alabama held ninth-ranked Auburn to just eighty yards of total offense and led 16–3 with less than six minutes to play. Then lightning struck—twice. The Tigers' Bill Newton blocked a pair of Alabama punts, and David Langner returned both for touchdowns, giving Auburn a stunning 17–16 victory. The game led to the now-famous Auburn rally chant: "Punt, 'Bama, Punt!" Alabama's final national championships under Bryant came in the 1978 and 1979 seasons, when the team lost only once in 24 games.

Bryant became the winningest coach in major college football (a record since broken by Joe Paterno and Eddie Robinson) when his 'Bama squad rallied for two late touchdowns in a thrilling, come-from-behind victory over Auburn in 1981. It was win number 315 for Bryant, and also the first coaching meeting between Bryant and Pat Dye, his former assistant who went on to win 99 games at Auburn. Bryant concluded his fabled Alabama career with 232 wins there (323 overall) and retired following the 1982 season. His teams won six national titles and 15 bowl games, and had four undefeated seasons. The Bear died at age 69 from heart failure on January 26, 1983, just 28 days after he had coached his final football game.

While the Crimson Tide dominated the series in the 1960s and '70s, the rivalry would reach new heights in the following decade. In 1982 Auburn snapped its nine-year losing skid to Alabama when another Auburn Heisman Trophy–winner, Bo Jackson, dove over the goal line from a yard away for the one-point victory. Auburn reeled off victories in six of eight games from

BO KNOWS TROPHIES: Auburn's Bo Jackson poses with his Heisman Trophy, 1985.

1982–89, including four in a row (1986–89). Highlights from those years were the 1985 game, when Alabama's place kicker Van Tiffin booted a 52-yard field goal as time expired to win, and 1986, when Auburn flanker Lawyer Tillman ran a reverse into the end zone with 32 seconds remaining for the winning touchdown.

All games had been played at Birmingham's Legion Field since the series was resumed in 1948. Despite Auburn's ambitious attempts to host Alabama, the Crimson Tide did not wish to make the cross-state journey to play at Auburn.

"It won't ever happen," predicted Alabama coach Ray Perkins.

On December 2, 1989, it did happen, when Alabama played at Jordan-Hare Stadium for the first time in the history of the rivalry. (The stadium is named for Auburn's winningest coach, Ralph "Shug" Jordan, and Clifford Hare, a member of the first football team.) Prior to the game, the Auburn players walked from the athletic dormitory to the football stadium past adoring fans lining the street to wish them good luck. This is an Auburn tradition called the Tiger Walk, and the 20,000 fans on Donahue Drive

STAT BOX

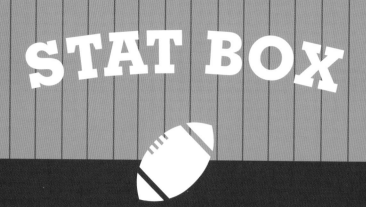

FIRST GAME

FEBRUARY 22, 1893 • AUBURN 32–ALABAMA 22

LIFETIME HEAD-TO-HEAD RECORD

ALABAMA 38–AUBURN 30 (1 TIE)

SERIES NICKNAME

THE IRON BOWL

NATIONAL CHAMPIONSHIPS

ALABAMA: 9	**AUBURN: 1**
1925, 1926, 1961, 1964, 1965, 1973, 1978, 1979, 1992	1957

HEISMAN TROPHY WINNERS

ALABAMA: 0	**AUBURN: 2**
	BO JACKSON (1985)
	PAT SULLIVAN (1971)

MOST LOPSIDED WIN

1948: ALABAMA 55–AUBURN 0

HOME FIELDS

ALABAMA: BRYANT-DENNY

AUBURN: JORDAN-HARE

that day are believed to be the largest Tiger Walk crowd ever. Alabama came into the game unbeaten with ten wins and was ranked No. 2 in the nation. Before a stadium record crowd of 85,319, Auburn ended Alabama's championship aspirations with a 30–20 victory.

The game rotated between the Auburn and Birmingham stadiums from 1993 to '99. Auburn completed a perfect 11-win season under rookie coach Terry Bowden with an improbable win over Alabama in 1993. Their starting quarterback Stan White was down on the Jordan-Hare Stadium turf with an injury, and the Tigers' dream of an undefeated season was in jeopardy of falling short. Trailing 14–5 with six minutes left in the third quarter, sophomore backup quarterback Patrick Nix was inserted into the game facing a fourth down and 15 yards to go at the Alabama 35-yard line. With no time to loosen up his throwing arm, Nix took the first snap and connected on a pass to receiver Frank Sanders for a touchdown,

propelling Auburn to a monumental 22–14 win. In 2000, the game was played in Tuscaloosa, Alabama's home, for the first time in 100 years.

At Alabama, the rally cry is "Roll Tide Roll." For fans wearing the orange and blue of Auburn, the rally cry is "War Eagle." (The legend of the origin of the War Eagle battle cry dates back to the 1864 Battle of the Wilderness in Virginia during the Civil War.) Auburn currently holds the edge in the series, having won four of the last five meetings through 2004, and seven of the last twelve. That accounts for what has looked like a toilet paper blizzard in the center of downtown Auburn, where College Street intersects Magnolia Avenue. There at Toomer's Corner, a local watering hole where the Auburn faithful meet to celebrate significant Tiger victories, they cover the trees with toilet paper, appropriating their rivals' call to "roll on."

—D.F.

GOING DOWN: Auburn's Hicks Poor tries to fight off Alabama safety Kelvin Sigler, 1997. In a close battle, Auburn beat the Crimson Tide, 18–17.

USC *vs.* NOTRE DAME

BLOOD FEUD? BACKYARD BRAWL? BORDER WAR? NOT EXACTLY. THE UNIVERSITY OF NOTRE DAME– UNIVERSITY OF SOUTHERN California rivalry is more redolent of an arranged marriage between royal families of allied nations than it is a football feud. It was admiration, not abomination, that sowed the seeds of college football's definitive intersectional rivalry.

The motivation behind this union of gridiron giants was a truly aristocratic one: self-interest. In 1925 the USC Trojans, a burgeoning powerhouse relegated to pummeling inferior opponents within a time zone or two, were seeking to "marry up"—they wanted national exposure. The Irish, or as they were more commonly known then, Rockne's Ramblers (after legendary coach Knute Rockne), were looking for a sunny reprieve from the churlish late-autumn Midwestern weather.

As the story goes, the Irish were in Lincoln, Nebraska, for a Thanksgiving 1925 game against the Cornhuskers. Notre Dame and Nebraska had played one another annually, and evenly, since 1915 (the Irish held a 5–4–1 edge). Southern Cal dispatched graduate manager Gwynn Wilson (the era's equivalent of an athletic director) and his wife, Marion, to the game in hopes of persuading Rockne to drop Nebraska, a school that had handed him three of his six losses in eight seasons, in favor of USC. Rockne was apprehensive; he considered the distance too far.

The Wilsons appealed to Rockne's missus, Bonnie. They took the train back to Chicago with the Irish, and during the trip persuaded Mrs. Rockne—who in turn persuaded her husband—that a biannual trip to sunny SoCal compared favorably to one to frigid Lincoln.

The following autumn, Nebraska was off the Notre Dame schedule and Southern Cal was on it. The first game, played December 4, 1926, in Los Angeles Memorial Coliseum, drew 105,000 fans. The Irish squeaked by the Trojans 13–12 on a 23-yard touchdown pass from Art Parisien to Johnny Niemiec.

The next year the Trojans made their first trek east of the Rockies and played the Irish at Soldier Field in Chicago. In front of 120,000 fans, the largest crowd ever to witness a college or pro football game in person, the Irish again won a nail-biter, 7–6.

The enormity of the crowds, fueled by the charisma of both schools and their coaches (Rockne of Notre Dame, Howard "Headman" Jones at USC), bore proof of the first great rivalry between East and West in college football. In 1931 in South Bend the Irish, winners of 26 straight games, entered the fourth quarter with a 14–0 lead. The boys from Troy clawed back, though, as Johnny Baker kicked the game-winning field goal with

---

THE BOYS FROM TROY CLAWED BACK AS JOHNNY BAKER KICKED THE GAME-WINNING FIELD GOAL WITH ONE MINUTE REMAINING.

ROCKNE AND HIS RAMBLERS: Fighting Irish coach Knute Rockne with his football team, 1930. At first hesitant to make the trip to USC, Rockne's wife convinced him.

one minute remaining. USC 16, Notre Dame 14. When the Trojans returned to Los Angeles, they were treated to a ticker-tape parade that drew more than 300,000.

Opposites attract: the cabin-fever Catholic school located amidst the flat farmland of northern Indiana versus the sun-splashed, surf's-up campus located just a traffic jam away from Hollywood and Malibu. But the rivalry has always meant more than that. It also involves two schools who more often than not have pitted national championship–caliber squads against one another. Two schools who, after eight decades, can trace some of their highest and lowest moments to games against the other. The marriage has history.

With the exception of three seasons during World War II, Southern Cal and Notre Dame have met every year since '26. In odd-numbered years the Trojans visit South Bend in October (although for the first few decades it was November); in even-numbered years, the Irish play their final game of the season against USC in Los Angeles. It's a tradition older than the Heisman Trophy, which, incidentally, has been won by a Notre Dame player seven times and by a Southern Cal player six. No school has more Heismans than these two.

Notre Dame leads the annual series 42–29–5, but

neither school has the definitive upper hand in this rivalry. Southern Cal has won 11 national championships; Notre Dame has won 12. Each school would likely have more had they never started this relationship. In 1964, 1970, and 1980, the Trojans handed the Irish their first season loss in the year's final game. In 1927, 1947, 1952, 1973, and 1988, Notre Dame was the only team to upend Southern Cal. Since the Associated Press poll began in 1936, the two have met 16 times when both were ranked in the top ten. In these years, USC won eight times, Notre Dame seven (with one tie).

Rockne, whom USC had actually attempted to hire away from Notre Dame prior to the 1925 season, was the series' first legend and mischief-maker. In 1930 Notre Dame, 9–0, stopped in Tucson, Arizona, to practice en route to its meeting against 8–1 USC. Rockne, mindful that L.A. sportswriters were viewing the workout, dressed his speedy halfback, Bucky O'Connor, in another player's jersey and ordered him to ease off. The ruse worked, and O'Connor ran under the radar. That contest, Rockne's last, found the coach at his indomitable and charming best. On the eve of the game he somehow wangled an invitation to speak at the Trojans' team banquet. Rockne played possum, humbly asking the Trojan players to congratulate his squad on their sportsmanship and effort after USC's victory the next day.

The Irish won the game, 27–0, and the national championship. O'Connor, "out of nowhere," scored three touchdowns, all of them on runs of 50 yards or more.

That item of trivia is one of many that former Notre Dame coach Lou Holtz included on his "USC Test." Holtz, who went 9–1–1 against the Trojans (suffering his lone loss, an overtime heartbreaker, in his last game as Irish coach in 1996), used to give his players a written exam on the USC–Notre Dame rivalry. If they failed, Holtz, who described the scope of the series as "international," made them retake it until they passed.

A QUICK STUDY GUIDE—WITHOUT EVER HAVING SEEN IT— TO THE USC TEST:

• **51-0:** In 1966 unranked USC spoiled Notre Dame coach Ara Parseghian's dream of a perfect debut season with two touchdowns in the final five minutes to win 20–17. The game-winner came on a fourth-down desperation pass from Craig Fertig to Rod Sherman with 1:33 left. Two years later Parseghian returned to the L.A. Coliseum

LOST CAUSE: The Notre Dame second string watches their team take a beating from USC.

with another unbeaten Notre Dame squad and whipped the Trojans 51–0. It remains the most lopsided loss in Southern Cal history.

•**ANTHONY DAVIS:** The splendid Trojan tailback scored 11 touchdowns in his career against the Irish, including six in a virtuoso performance in 1972 when the top-ranked Trojans beat the Irish, 45–23. However, it was his effort two years later in the Coliseum that cemented his name as a household term in both Irish and Trojan abodes.

Notre Dame, boasting the nation's No. 1 defense, exited the field at halftime with a 24–0 lead. Davis fielded the second-half kickoff and raced it back virtually unchallenged for a touchdown. It seemed as if Davis never did stop running, as the Trojans retaliated with an unfathomable 55 unanswered points. In a game that all Trojan fans refer to simply as "the Comeback," USC won 55–24, led by Davis' four touchdowns.

STAT BOX

FIRST GAME

DECEMBER 4, 1926 • NOTRE DAME 13–USC 12

LIFETIME HEAD-TO-HEAD RECORD

NOTRE DAME 42–USC 29 (5 TIES)

NATIONAL CHAMPIONSHIPS

USC: 11

1928, 1931, 1932, 1939, 1962, 1967, 1972, 1974, 1978, 2003, 2004

NOTRE DAME: 12

1924, 1929, 1930, 1943, 1946, 1947, 1949, 1953, 1966, 1973, 1977, 1988

HEISMAN TROPHY WINNERS

USC: 6

MIKE GARRETT (1965)

O.J. SIMPSON (1968)

CHARLES WHITE (1979)

MARCUS ALLEN (1981)

CARSON PALMER (2002)

MATT LEINART (2004)

NOTRE DAME: 7

ANGELO BERTELLI (1943)

JOHNNY LUJACK (1947)

LEON HART (1949)

JOHN LATTNER (1953)

PAUL HORNUNG (1956)

JOHN HUARTE (1964)

TIM BROWN (1987)

MOST LOPSIDED WIN

NOTRE DAME WHOMPED USC BY 51 POINTS IN 1966

THE DIFFERENT SPHERES OF USC AND NOTRE DAME

USC	NOTRE DAME
METHODIST	CATHOLIC
URBAN	SUBURBAN
WEST COAST	MIDWEST
CARDINAL AND GOLD	BLUE AND GOLD
ANIMAL MASCOT (TRAVELER THE HORSE)	HUMANOID MASCOT (LEPRECHAUN)
CONFERENCE MEMBER (PAC 10)	INDEPENDENT
OFF-CAMPUS PUBLIC STADIUM	ON-CAMPUS PRIVATE STADIUM
11 NATIONAL TITLES (2ND ALL-TIME)	12 NATIONAL TITLES (1ST ALL-TIME)
6 HEISMAN WINNERS (2ND ALL-TIME)	7 HEISMAN WINNERS (1ST ALL-TIME)

Curiously enough, the Trojans produced four Heisman Trophy–winning tailbacks between 1965–1981 (Mike Garrett, O. J. Simpson, Charles White, and Marcus Allen), but Davis was not among them. Don't tell that to the Irish.

•GREEN JERSEYS: In 1977 Notre Dame donned green jerseys for the first time in 14 years and throttled No. 5 Southern Cal 49–19. The Irish had gone through pregame warmups in their regular home blue jerseys. Minutes later, a replica Trojan horse was wheeled onto the field. Four Irish captains climbed out from within

it, wearing the emerald-green shirts. The rest of the "Green Machine," huddled in the tunnel, followed them out, sending Notre Dame Stadium into bedlam. The Irish, who entered the midseason contest ranked 11th, would win the national championship (USC won it the following year).

•0:02: Time remaining when USC's Frank Jordan kicked a 37-yard field goal for a 27–25 Trojan victory in 1978.

•0:00: Time remaining when Notre Dame's John Carney kicked a 19-yard field goal for a 38–37 Irish victory in 1986.

HAVE A SEAT: A Trojan goes in for the tackle as Notre Dame fights to stay alive, 1988. Notre Dame triumphed in the end, on the way to its most recent national title.

USC VS.
UCLA

While some Trojans consider Notre Dame their school's biggest rival, others look much closer to home—approximately ten miles crosstown, to be specific—in ranking UCLA as Public Enemy Number One.

The fight for city bragging rights often plays out within families: It's often brother against brother, sister against sister, or friend against friend. And the taunts get passed down through generations. Bruins love nothing more than referring to USC as the University of Spoiled Children. Trojans love to counter with this one-liner: What does a UCLA graduate call a USC graduate? Boss.

The schools first met in 1929 and over time have turned a local brawl into a game of national importance. Between them, they have produced seven Heisman Trophy winners, 12 national championships, and 26 Rose Bowl champions.

America's only major intra-city college sports rivalry is so fierce it even has a corporate sponsor. Since 2001, the school with the most successful year against the other, based on points from the 18 total sports competed in, receives the Lexus Gauntlet award. No matter who wins the award, when the Bruins and Trojans compete, the result is ecstasy on one side, misery on the other.

—John Clendening

•1988: This was the only year that the Notre Dame–Southern Cal match-up was a No. 1 vs. No. 2. The Trojans entered the Los Angeles Coliseum (packed with 93,829 fans) with a 10–0 record and the nation's No. 2 ranking. The Irish charged in with an identical record and a higher position in the polls, but minus two of its best running backs, Tony Brooks and Ricky Watters. The two talented sophomores had arrived late to a team dinner the night before and by Saturday's kickoff were already headed on a plane back to South Bend.

Thanks to a suffocating defense, however, and the play of quarterback Tony Rice, the Irish prevailed 27–10 and went on to win the national title.

•PRIME-TIME HEISMANS: In 2002 and 2004, the Trojans hosted the Irish in prime-time on Saturday evening in nationally televised games. Each time, USC's quarterback entered the game as a Heisman trophy candidate, though not necessarily a lock to win the award. In '02 Trojan Carson Palmer threw for 425 yards and four touchdowns, setting all-time records for a Notre Dame opponent, as Southern Cal won 44–13. Palmer went on to win the Heisman.

In 2004 Matt Leinart threw for 400 yards and five touchdowns in a 41–10 rout. Leinart also would win the Heisman, making it two in three seasons that a Trojan quarterback had won college football's most coveted award, an oddity at Tailback U.

By the way, the combined score of the second halves of those two games is enough to make an Irish fan nauseous: USC 47, Notre Dame 0.

Those are only a few of the memorable moments in college football's greatest intersectional rivalry. From Montana (Joe) to Marinovich (Todd), from White (Charles) to Brown (Tim), this has always been a rich rivalry and yet one of mutual suspect. Consider this final point: The quarterback of that Southern Cal team that ravaged the Irish for 55 unanswered points in 1974 was Pat Haden. Today Haden is a commentator on NBC's national broadcasts of Notre Dame home football games.

—JOHN WALTERS

Notre Dame grad John Walters is currently a reporter at *SI on Campus*, after writing and reporting for *Sports Illustrated* for a dozen years. He is the author of several books, including *Same River Twice* and *Basketball for Dummies* (coauthor).

HEISMAN POSE: USC quarterback Matt Leinart sets to throw for a touchdown in a game against Notre Dame, 2004. USC won 41–10, and Leinart won the Heisman.

DODGERS *vs.* GIANTS

THEY'RE AS DIFFERENT AS UPPER MANHATTAN AND FLATBUSH, AS NORTH BEACH AND VENICE BEACH, AS MARKET Street and Sunset Boulevard. They're as competitive as Durocher and Robinson, as Marichal and Roseboro, as Bonds and Gagne. No wonder the Giants and Dodgers have been at each other's throats since the first time they met.

They've been an unusually well-matched pair. Through 116 years of mostly controlled mayhem in New York and Brooklyn, and then San Francisco and Los Angeles, the Giants and Dodgers have each won 18 National League pennants. The Dodgers have won six World Series, the Giants five. The Giants beat the Dodgers 1,040 times, and the Dodgers returned the favor 1,016 times. In incidents separated by six decades and 3,000 miles, two Giants fans were murdered by Dodgers fans in altercations directly traceable to the heat of the rivalry. (Given the closeness

> ## "IT WAS LIKE A WAR EVERY TIME WE PLAYED THE GIANTS"
> ## —PEE WEE REESE, DODGER

of all the other stats, Dodgers fans had better watch their backs.) Said Pee Wee Reese, captain of the Dodgers' legendary teams of the 1950s, "It was like a war every time we played the Giants."

Hostilities commenced on October 18, 1889, at the Polo Grounds near the banks of the Harlem River. Although the New York Giants and the franchise that would become the Brooklyn Dodgers were both founded in 1883, they played in different leagues—and in different cities, as New York's five boroughs would not become consolidated into what is today the Big Apple until 1898. When the N.L. champion Giants and the American Association champion Brooklyn Bridegrooms were introduced

in a nine-game precursor to the World Series, Brooklyn won three of four, then dropped five in a row.

Within a few years the Brooklyn team would become the Trolley Dodgers, a derisive nickname bestowed by Giants fans that was quickly embraced. Brooklyn fans hurled plenty of derision of their own, not to mention bottles, coins, and assorted trash aimed at the Giants as they traveled over the Brooklyn Bridge in horse-drawn carriages.

"Brooklyn was the borough of immigrants, of trolley cars, of ordinary buildings and ordinary lives," the Dodgers' Hall of Fame broadcaster, Vin Scully, has said. "If you came from Brooklyn, you were the butt of jokes. Manhattan, with its lordly spires and tall buildings, was seen as superior, and that built up a lot of resentment in people from Brooklyn."

Led by the pugnacious John McGraw, the Giants ruled the early years. In 1914 ex-Giants coach Wilbert "Uncle Robbie" Robinson crossed the East River to join the Dodgers as their manager. Uncle Robbie directed the Dodgers to two pennants, but the boomlet didn't last. With the Dodgers tucked away in the second division each fall, Giants manager Bill Terry felt safe enough to make a joke at their expense in 1934. Asked about the Dodgers' chances, Terry responded with mock incredulity: "Brooklyn? Is Brooklyn still in the league?" He found out in the final weekend of the season, when the sixth-place Dodgers rose up to knock the Giants out of the race.

As Robert W. Creamer wrote in *Baseball in '41*, "About

GLAD-HANDING THE ENEMY: Giants manager John McGraw shakes hands with Dodger coach Wilbert "Uncle Robbie" Robinson, 1924.

the only time the Dodgers seemed important was when they were playing the Giants. In the old eight-team league, teams played each other 22 times a year, and the Dodgers and Giants played each other 22 times in the same city . . . The Giants usually dominated, but any Dodger victory at any time was a sweet vindication, a spasm of triumph, for Brooklynites."

But with the arrival of general managers Larry McPhail and, later, Branch Rickey, the Dodgers gradually built a perennial contender that would later become known, thanks to author Roger Kahn, as the "Boys of Summer." It was during this era that the battle was truly joined. The Dodgers and Giants won eight of ten pennants between 1947 and 1956 (six for the Dodgers, two for the Giants). Not coincidentally, the teams were the first two in the N.L. to integrate; Jackie Robinson blazed a trail with the Dodgers in 1947, and Monte Irvin and Hank Thompson

joined the Giants in '49. (On July 8 of that year, when Thompson stood in against the Dodgers' rookie Don Newcombe, it was the first time an African-American hitter had faced an African-American pitcher on a big-league stage.)

By 1951, the Dodgers were the class of the league—or so it seemed to their manager, Chuck Dressen, who proclaimed "the Giants are dead" in April and boldly opened a door between the two teams' clubhouses to heckle them after an August sweep. Dressen didn't realize it until October, but he'd actually opened the door to the greatest comeback in baseball history. The Giants won 16 in a row, and 37 of their last 44, to make up 13 ½ games and force a three-game playoff versus the Dodgers for the pennant.

The teams split the first two games. In Game Three at the Polo Grounds, the Dodgers held a 4–2 lead with

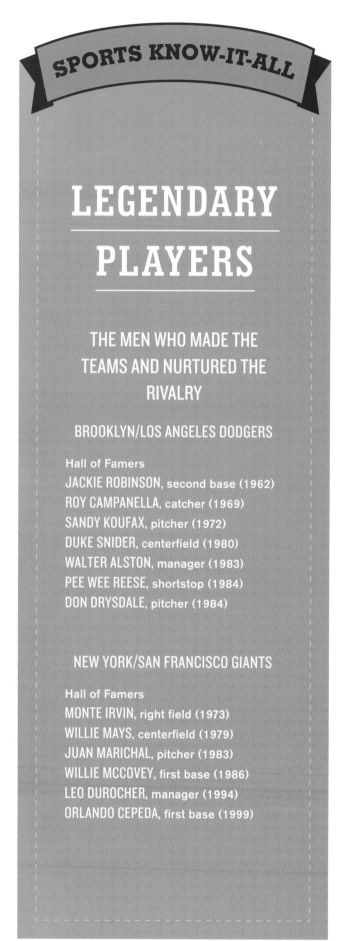

LEGENDARY PLAYERS

THE MEN WHO MADE THE TEAMS AND NURTURED THE RIVALRY

BROOKLYN/LOS ANGELES DODGERS

Hall of Famers
JACKIE ROBINSON, second base (1962)
ROY CAMPANELLA, catcher (1969)
SANDY KOUFAX, pitcher (1972)
DUKE SNIDER, centerfield (1980)
WALTER ALSTON, manager (1983)
PEE WEE REESE, shortstop (1984)
DON DRYSDALE, pitcher (1984)

NEW YORK/SAN FRANCISCO GIANTS

Hall of Famers
MONTE IRVIN, right field (1973)
WILLIE MAYS, centerfield (1979)
JUAN MARICHAL, pitcher (1983)
WILLIE MCCOVEY, first base (1986)
LEO DUROCHER, manager (1994)
ORLANDO CEPEDA, first base (1999)

one out in the bottom of the ninth, but it was far from secure. The Giants had runners on second and third when outfielder Bobby Thomson, who'd hit .427 down the stretch, walked to the plate. Willie Mays, then a 20-year-old phenom, was in the on-deck circle, worrying that the Dodgers would have reliever Ralph Branca walk Thomson to get to him. But that was not Dressen's plan. Thomson would get his chance. "If you've ever hit one," Giants manager Leo Durocher howled from the third-base coaching box, "hit it now!"

Thomson took a strike, then connected with a curve-ball low and away. It rocketed on a line into the lower deck, just above the 315-foot sign, to give the Giants a 5–4 win. Giants broadcaster Russ Hodges rose to the occasion with this memorable call: "There's a long drive . . . it's gonna be . . . I believe . . . the Giants win the pennant! The Giants win the pennant! The Giants win the pennant! The Giants win the pennant! I don't believe it! The Giants win the pennant!"

The dramatic finish (courtesy of perhaps the most famous home run in baseball history; see box on page 87) earned the Giants the right to lose to the Yankees in the World Series, but that didn't make the Dodgers feel

STEALING HISTORY: Dodger infielder Jackie Robinson scores against the Giants.

THE GIANTS WIN THE PENNANT!: An elated Giants team mobs Bobby Thomson after his home run off reliever Ralph Branca (bottom right) clinches the pennant, 1951.

"IF YOU'VE EVER HIT ONE, HIT IT NOW!"
— GIANTS MANAGER LEO DUROCHER

any better. In fact, it ignited a beanball war and a series of sometimes violent skirmishes that flared on and off for decades. In 1952 two different Giants pitchers hit Dodgers outfielder Carl Furillo. The second time it happened, Furillo motioned for Durocher to come out and fight. Durocher responded with a gesture of his own, and Furillo rushed the dugout, touching off a brawl. "We didn't like them, and they didn't like us," Thomson later said. Added Dodgers infielder Don Zimmer, "We disliked the Giants a lot more than the Yankees." As if to prove the point, Jackie Robinson retired rather than

join the Giants when he was traded to that club following the 1956 season.

That was the beginning of the end for the New York portion of the feud. Two years later the Giants and Dodgers both fled their antiquated urban stadiums in pursuit of greater wealth on the West Coast. The Dodgers took Los Angeles, and the Giants set up shop 450 miles north in San Francisco. They brought the old grudges along with them. In fact, most of the best races in the history of the rivalry came after the Great Relocation.

In 1959 the Giants led the Dodgers by three games

on September 6, but the Dodgers finished 15–5 and swept the Giants in the final series to win the pennant. Three years later the Giants took revenge, winning a three-game playoff for the 1962 pennant almost as dramatically as they had in 1951. First, manager Bill Rigney ordered the groundskeepers at Candlestick Park to flood the basepaths, slowing the Dodgers' record-setting basestealer, Maury Wills. "There wasn't a cloud in the sky," Hall of Fame broadcaster Scully remembered. "And the infield was drowned." The Giants won the first game, 8–0.

"We were so angry over the mud that we couldn't concentrate at the plate," Wills said. They recovered to take a wild Game Two, 8–7, at Dodger Stadium. In the third game, the Dodgers brought a 4–2 lead into the top of the ninth, but relievers Ed Roebuck and Stan Williams melted down, giving up two singles, four walks, and a wild pitch. The Giants happily came away with a 6–4 victory and the pennant, 11 years to the day after Thomson's "Shot Heard 'Round the World." Completing the symmetry, they again met their match in the World Series, falling to the Yankees in seven games.

The ugliest moment involving these two teams, and one of the ugliest moments in American sports history, played out against the backdrop of the pennant race in 1965. On Aug. 22, Giants starter Juan Marichal sent two Dodgers spinning into the dirt with inside pitches. When Marichal came to the plate in the bottom of the third, Dodgers catcher John Roseboro buzzed a return

UNSPORTSMANLIKE CONDUCT: Dodger Sandy Koufax tries to break up a fight between Giants starter Juan Marichal and Dodgers' John Roseboro, 1965. The brawl lasted nearly 15 minutes.

BRANCA AND THOMSON

On the afternoon of October 3, 1951, it was inconceivable that the two men might someday be pals. But here they are, in the 21st century, speaking at charity events, signing autographs at card shows, sometimes even singing a song written for them by a couple of pressbox cranks.

Ralph Branca served up the most famous gopher ball in baseball history. Bobby Thomson hit it out of the park. The Giants win the pennant! Branca pitched a few more years in the big leagues and then opened an insurance office in White Plains, New York. He ultimately became a champion fundraiser for the Baseball Assistance Team, which benefits indigent ex-ballplayers, and his daughter married former Mets and Rangers manager Bobby Valentine. Thomson made it into the '60s as a player, then earned a comfortable living as a paper products salesman in Watchung, New Jersey.

As the years passed and the anniversary of the famous homer kept rolling around, Branca resisted taking part. Eventually he relented, and a curious thing happened. He and Thomson discovered they liked each other. "I guess you could say the trauma has diminished," Branca said. "Bobby and I have been good friends for years. He's a good guy. I probably talk to him more than I do any other ex-ballplayer."

"I think he did take it kind of hard at first," Thomson said. "But he gradually came to accept it. And let's face it. Without that moment, we'd both be long forgotten."

throw to pitcher Sandy Koufax that ticked Marichal's right ear. "If I had turned my head it would have hit me in the face," Marichal later said. "Nobody has to throw a ball that close and that hard . . . I looked back. I asked him, 'Why did you do that?' He moved two steps toward me and he said, '— you.' "

Enraged, Marichal raised his bat and struck Roseboro on the head. The ensuing brawl lasted nearly 15 minutes, and it took 14 stitches to close the gash above the catcher's left eyebrow—catchers of the day did not wear the helmets worn today. Although the Giants' ace was only suspended for eight days, it cost him two starts. The Giants held a four-game lead with 12 to play, but the Dodgers went 11–1 and won the pennant by two games. (Marichal and Roseboro eventually reconciled, and as Roseboro lay dying in a hospital bed in 2002, Marichal

called to say he was praying for him.)

The Giants of Marichal, Mays, and Willie McCovey challenged the Dodgers of Koufax and Don Drysdale again in 1966, falling short by a game and a half. It was the Giants' turn in 1971, as they edged the Dodgers by a game for the N.L. West crown. Sparks flew in 1972, when Giants manager Charlie Fox and Dodgers coach Tommy Lasorda got into a fistfight at home plate during a pregame exchange of lineup cards.

The Dodgers were ascendant and the Giants dormant for much of the '70s, nearly bolting for Toronto at one point. By 1982 they were competitive again, battling to the last days of a three-team race with the Dodgers and the Braves. First, the Dodgers eliminated the Giants, and then the Giants returned the gesture in the final game.

STAT BOX

FIRST GAME

OCTOBER 18, 1889

LIFETIME HEAD-TO-HEAD RECORD

GIANTS 1,040–DODGERS 1,016

WORLD SERIES TITLES

DODGERS: 6	GIANTS: 5
1955, 1959, 1963, 1965, 1981, 1988	1905, 1921, 1922, 1933, 1954

LARGEST CROWDS

61,756 (DODGERS AT GIANTS, MAY 30, 1937)

55,185 (GIANTS AT DODGERS, JULY 28, 1973)

HOME PARKS

GIANTS: POLO GROUNDS (FORMER); SBC PARK (CURRENT)

DODGERS: EBBETS FIELD (FORMER); DODGER STADIUM (CURRENT)

BEST AND WORST SEASON RECORD

DODGERS	GIANTS
BEST: 1953, 105–49	**BEST:** 1885, 85–27
.682 (1ST PLACE)	.759 (2 GAMES BACK)
WORST: 1905, 48–104	**WORST:** 1902, 48–88
.316 (56.5 GAMES BACK)	.353 (53.5 GAMES BACK)

The two teams took turns spoiling each other's hopes in 1991 (Giants eliminate Dodgers, who finish one game back of the Braves) and 1993 (Dodgers eliminate Giants, who win 103 games but still finish one game back of, you guessed it, the Braves). The Dodgers also knocked the Giants out of the race in 2001, with a 12–1 spanking that put the Arizona Diamondbacks into the playoffs, and sucker-punched them on the next-to-last day of the 2004 season, scoring seven runs in the bottom of the ninth to win 7–3 and clinch the West. "We do it the Hollywood way, that's for sure," said closer Eric Gagne. "It's amazing."

As the rivalry steams toward its 13th decade, it's as heated as it ever was. Whatever you may have heard about late-arriving, traffic-beating Dodgers fans, or wine-sipping, foggy-headed Giants fans, forget about it. When these two teams play, obscene chants reverberate through stately Dodger Stadium, and the crowds at waterfront SBC Park roar: "Beat L.A."

In these days of widespread player movement, it's not uncommon for guys on one team to have played for the other. When longtime Giants second baseman Jeff Kent returned to San Francisco in 2005 for his first

FAMOUS WORDS

"Brooklyn? Is Brooklyn still in the league?"
—*Giants manager Bill Terry poking fun at the down-and-out Dodgers, 1934*

"The Giants are dead."
—*Dodgers manager Chuck Dressen on the down-and-out Giants, 1951*

"There's a long drive . . . it's gonna be . . . I believe . . . the Giants win the pennant! The Giants win the pennant! The Giants win the pennant! The Giants win the pennant! I don't believe it! The Giants win the pennant!"
—*Giants broadcaster Russ Hodges on Bobby Thomson's game-winning homer against the Dodgers known as "the shot heard 'round the world," 1951*

WHICH TEAM ARE YOU ON?: Ex-Giant second baseman Jeff Kent tries to complete a double play.

series wearing Dodger blue, Giants fans had just the right response: "BOOOOO!" (Kent was hardly devastated; he went 6-for-11.)

The players may not despise each other the way they used to—not all the time, anyway—but they feed off the energy of the other team's fans. "It's great knowing how much they hate you," said outfielder Brett Butler, a Giant and Dodger in the 1980s and '90s. "You love it. This is the kind of rivalry baseball needs. It's lasted a long time, and let's hope it lasts for a long time to come."

—JON SCHER

Jon Scher is the baseball editor of *ESPN The Magazine.* He formerly worked at *Sports Illustrated* and *Baseball America.*

HARVARD vs. YALE

THROUGH THE HALLOWED HALLS OF HARVARD AND YALE HAVE TROOPED THE MEN (AND NOW WOMEN) WHO HAVE LED America for nearly 300 years. Presidents, generals, leaders of industry, ambassadors, writers, scientists, scholars—the two schools have produced more than their fair share of leaders and standard-setters. The brick and ivy walls of Harvard and the marble hallways of Yale have witnessed just about every kind of scene in American history, from the Revolution forward.

But more importantly as far as alumni are concerned, every November the two schools meet head-to-head in a football game. Nobel Prizes and Oval Offices are nice, but what really matters is winning "The Game."

Football players for Harvard and Yale have been knocking heads for 130 years. There are older football rivalries, such as Amherst–Williams and Lafayette–Lehigh, and rivalries that draw more national attention, including Ohio State–Michigan or Auburn–Alabama. But no other college football rivalry is so pivotal to the history of the sport itself. Played in New England each year on the third Saturday in November, The Game, as it is haughtily known, has been played 121 times, through 2004, with Yale holding the edge in the series, 64–49–8.

During the early decades of college football, the Harvard Crimson and the Yale Bulldogs were dominant powers, and their annual meeting represented the clash of the two most successful teams around. The pair combined to win 18 of the first 36 national championships—and have won none since 1919. While the schools no longer

> ## THE PAIR COMBINED TO WIN 18 OF THE FIRST 36 NATIONAL CHAMPIONSHIPS—AND HAVE WON NONE SINCE 1919.

field championship caliber teams, their annual face-off still resonates among its fans with a significance unequaled in college sports. A college football rivalry, after all, is only as good as the grudge held by its rabid fans. The players move on after graduation, changing the team's makeup from year to year. But the loyal and dedicated faithful who are the alumni have staying power, rooting for an institution and cheering for a uniform like zealous patriots saluting the flag.

The hard feelings began on November 13, 1875, when Ulysses S. Grant held the office of the presidency and football was in its infancy. Fifteen players on each team tried to kick a ball across the opponent's goal line, in a game played mostly using feet. The first Harvard–Yale football game was played with these soccer-like rules. Harvard won, 4–0, at Hamilton Park in Connecticut. Later that night while singing "With Crimson in Triumph Flashing," seven Harvard boosters who had journeyed by carriage from Cambridge were arrested for disturbing the peace and each fined five dollars.

That initial football meeting attracted more than 2,000 fans, a huge crowd for the day, so the two schools decided to make the gridiron match-up an annual event. (The beginning of the Harvard–Yale athletic rivalry actually began more than two decades earlier, in August 1852, when Harvard crew won a two-mile rowing race on New Hampshire's Lake Winnipesaukee.) The football rivalry

AN IVY LEAGUE RUMBLE: The annual Harvard–Yale game, 1960. "The Game" has been fought for 130 years.

FOUNDING FATHERS: Walter Camp (second row center, with laced shirt) and William Heffelfinger (top row, second from right) pose with the rest of Yale's football team, 1901.

heated up as the sport evolved into modified rugby (picking up the ball and running with it until getting tackled was permitted) by the end of the century. No helmets or any protective equipment had been adopted; the players wore hats, knickers, and britches for uniforms. The brutal battles continued, notably the 1894 game in Springfield, Massachusetts, called the "Bloodbath in Hampsden Park" due to the Crimson's use of the controversial flying wedge, a momentum play in which the blocking linemen form a solid wall of interference by locking arms and getting a running start. It was a dangerous play, as a Yale player found out the hard way. He was carried off the field and was thought to have died in the locker room. As it turned out, he only suffered a "contusion of the brain" and returned to play again. The flying wedge was soon outlawed because of its brutality, but not before the alarming injury rate had caused a two-year break in football relations between the schools. The learned Harvard faculty attempted to ban the objectionable sport from campus altogether. The inherently violent game, wrote

the deans of Harvard, "is brutal, demoralizing to teams and spectators, and extremely dangerous."

Leading the way in making the game safer and more dignified was Walter Camp, a player and coach at Yale, who would become known as the "Father of American Football." Camp came up with changes that turned English rugby into the game of American football as we know it today. He created the ideas for a line of scrimmage, the center snap, 11 men per side, and downs and yards to gain. Using the center snap instead of the rugby scrum let the offense run set plays and use strategy, but the severe injury toll continued to mount.

On the Yale side, several personalities of this era stand out. One of Yale's first stars was William "Pudge" Heffelfinger, the three-time All-America guard who would become the first professional football player when he was paid $500 dollars by a Pennsylvania team in 1892. Another was the first two-sport star, Amos Alonzo Stagg, who played in Dr. James Naismith's first organized basketball game in 1891 and is the only person elected to both college football and basketball Halls of Fame. Together, they helped Yale to win eight of the first 12 college football titles from 1883 to '94, and the Elis (a popular nickname for Yale students) would add three more titles by 1909. Yale fans had opportunity to sing numerous choruses of their favorite fight songs, including "Boola Boola" and "Bingo, That's the Lingo" the latter written in 1910 by Cole Porter (Yale class of 1913), who went on to do pretty well in the song business.

Harvard won the national title in undefeated seasons in 1890 and consecutively in 1898 and '99. Percy Haughton became head coach in 1908 and created a Crimson dynasty lasting until World War I. Led by running back Charlie Brickley, Haughton's teams collected three national titles between 1910 and '13 and defeated Yale four straight times during that span. Harvard made its first and last postseason football appearance in the Rose Bowl on January 1, 1920, with coach Bob Fisher's Crimson squad edging Oregon, 7–6, in the Tournament of Roses contest at Pasadena for Harvard's seventh and last national title. In 1922 Harvard and Yale made an agreement not to enter postseason contests, feeling that the spectacle of such bowl games detracted too much from their educational mission. Of course, by not playing any games after The Game each year, they only enriched and emphasized the competition between them.

The Bulldogs and Crimson played to a stalemate in the 23 years between world wars (1919 to 1942), with Harvard holding only a two game edge. Yale dominated during the 1930s with six wins, three by shutout. Two Bulldogs who made a permanent mark in the record books were end Larry Kelley and halfback Clint Frank, two of the first three Heisman Trophy recipients (1936–37). Though the Ivy League has not had a Heisman Trophy winner since, Yale is one of only three schools with back-to-back trophy winners.

The Ivy League was established in 1956, and Harvard–Yale quickly became the marquee match-up of this conference of elite academic schools. Twenty times since then, The Game has decided the Ivy championship.

One of those games sums up not only the rivalry itself, but in many ways the importance of Harvard–Yale to college football history.

It has been called one of the most miraculous comebacks in collegiate football history. Harvard and Yale were vying for the Ivy League title. Going into the game, each

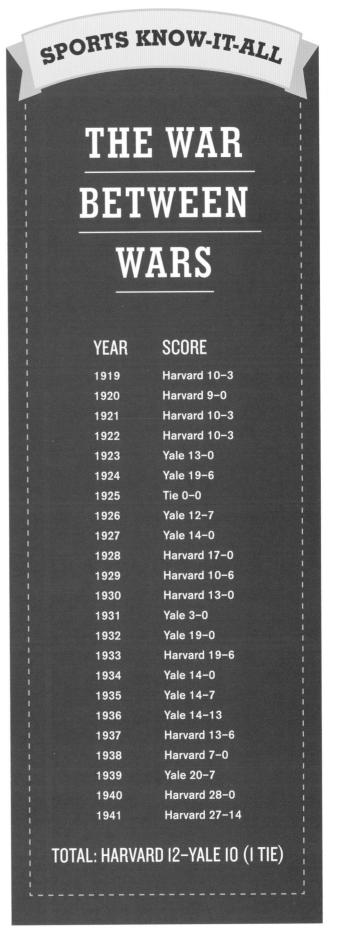

SPORTS KNOW-IT-ALL

THE WAR BETWEEN WARS

YEAR	SCORE
1919	Harvard 10–3
1920	Harvard 9–0
1921	Harvard 10–3
1922	Harvard 10–3
1923	Yale 13–0
1924	Yale 19–6
1925	Tie 0–0
1926	Yale 12–7
1927	Yale 14–0
1928	Harvard 17–0
1929	Harvard 10–6
1930	Harvard 13–0
1931	Yale 3–0
1932	Yale 19–0
1933	Harvard 19–6
1934	Yale 14–0
1935	Yale 14–7
1936	Yale 14–13
1937	Harvard 13–6
1938	Harvard 7–0
1939	Yale 20–7
1940	Harvard 28–0
1941	Harvard 27–14

TOTAL: HARVARD 12–YALE 10 (1 TIE)

HOAX OF
THE
CENTURY

Harvard's crushing 35–3 defeat over archrival Yale in the 121st football meeting between the two schools should have been the Crimson's time to shine. The victory capped an undefeated 2004 season and the Ivy League championship for the Crimson, and for the first time in eight decades Harvard had beaten Yale for a fourth straight time.

But all their successes were an afterthought to the ingenious prank carried out in the stands by a group of 20 Yale fans. These sly Bulldog supporters had painted their faces Crimson red and dressed up as a phony Harvard Pep Squad. With megaphones in hand, the Yalies ran up and down the aisles of Harvard Stadium in Cambridge, Massachusetts, encouraging the crowd to hold up the red and white placards that had been surreptitiously placed under their seats before the game. The 1,800 pieces of construction paper would spell out "Go Harvard," they said. Instead, every time a Harvard player excelled on the field (and that was often) the hometown fans held up their signs and spelled out "We Suck" in giant block letters for the whole stadium to see.

VICTORY SMILES: The Crimson team celebrates their win after the 2004 game, reveling in an undefeated season and the Ivy League championship.

STAT BOX

FIRST GAME

NOVEMBER 13, 1875 • HARVARD 4–YALE 0

LIFETIME HEAD-TO-HEAD RECORD

YALE 64–HARVARD 49 (8 TIES)

NATIONAL CHAMPIONSHIPS

HARVARD: 7

1890, 1898, 1899, 1910, 1912, 1913, 1919

YALE: 11

1883, 1884, 1886, 1887, 1888, 1891, 1892, 1894, 1900, 1907, 1909

HEISMAN TROPHY WINNERS

HARVARD: 0

YALE: 2

LARRY KELLEY (1936)

CLINT FRANK (1937)

MOST LOPSIDED WIN

YALE WHOMPED HARVARD 54–0 IN 1957

(BUT HARVARD BEAT YALE 41–0 IN 1915)

HOME FIELDS

HARVARD: HARVARD STADIUM

YALE: YALE BOWL

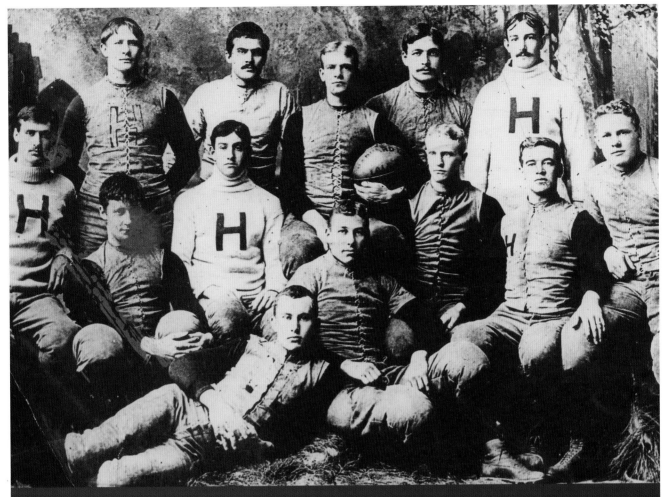

REAL MEN DON'T WEAR HELMETS: An early Harvard football team poses, 1890. Players usually wore only hats, knickers, and britches as uniforms in the early days of the rivalry.

team had won eight and lost none. It was the first time in 59 years the two schools had gone into their traditional game with each having perfect records to that point in the season. Featuring future NFL All-Pro running back Calvin Hill and quarterback Brian Dowling (the inspiration for the football helmet–wearing character B. D. in Gary Trudeau's "Doonesbury" comic strip), coach Carm Cozza's Yale squad had won 16 games in a row and was ranked No. 19 in the nation. Tommy Lee Jones, who would go on to star in blockbuster films such as *JFK* and *The Fugitive*, was an All-Ivy offensive tackle for the Crimson that season.

For 59 minutes and 18 seconds, the game was a very one-sided affair. Yale was leading, 29–13, and the visiting Yale faithful were proudly waving their white handkerchiefs and shouting, "You're Number 2!" That's when Harvard substitute quarterback Frank Champi, a balding 20-year-old junior history major, rallied his troops. With

42 seconds left on the clock, the Crimson accomplished the unimaginable: Champi (what better name for the hero?) passed for two touchdown scores and two two-point conversions to tie the Bulldogs as time ran out. Both teams shared the Ivy League title, and the gleeful headline in the Harvard student newspaper the next day declared: "Harvard Wins, 29–29."

Yale and Harvard, along with the rest of the Ivy League, moved to Division I-AA in 1982, signaling the decline of the once-national powers. Without scholarships, the Ivies are no longer able to attract the level of talented players that the superpower schools do. Although the meaning of the Harvard–Yale game has diminished with regard to its impact on the national college football landscape, to tens of thousands of students and alumni who care more about board scores than scoreboards, it is still the only game each year that really matters.

—D.F.

BEARS vs. PACKERS

IF THERE WERE A LOGO FOR THIS RIVALRY, IT WOULD BE A FIST. IF THERE WERE A SLOGAN FOR THIS RIVALRY, IT WOULD be unprintable. If there were a look for this rivalry, it would be a sneer . . . an ugly one.

The Green Bay Packers and the Chicago Bears have stared each other down 169 times since 1921 in a pro football rivalry without parallel in longevity and acrimony.

Over eight and a half decades of NFL warfare, the Packers and the Bears haven't always had good teams, and they seemingly haven't always been well matched. But year in and year out they've always wanted to knock each other's block off.

Lee Remmel can attest to that. As beat writer, publicist, and executive for the Packers for six decades, Remmel has seen 116 Packers–Bears games.

"There were many years in the past when Packer fans would have been happy if their team had won only two games in that year," Remmel said. "The two against those dreaded Bears."

Three stories from three eras—the beginning, the middle, and the recent past . . .

THE BEGINNING . . .

The rivalry started, appropriately, with a sucker punch and a broken nose. In 1921, when the Bears still were named after a Decatur, Illinois, starch company (the Staleys became the Bears in 1922), Chicago routed its town team neighbor from the north 20–0. And when no one was looking, least of all an official, Staleys guard Tarzan Taylor delivered an inside punch to the nose of Packers tackle Cub Buck in the second quarter. Of course, not many players wore helmets then, and of course Buck kept playing, vowing, not so silently, that he would turn Tarzan into Jane. It didn't happen.

In that 1920 game, the Staleys' owner/coach/end, a man named George Halas, scored his team's last touchdown, in the fourth quarter. A year earlier, when Halas was 25, you could have put another title in front of the slashes—league founder. Halas brought a disparate group of men together in a Hupmobile (an automobile of the time) showroom in Canton, Ohio, to form what soon would become the National Football League.

THE MIDDLE . . .

Four decades later, George Halas, leader of the Monsters of the Midway in the forties and fifties, had become known as Papa Bear.

He was loved and he was hated and sometimes the allegiances that built those emotions were blurred.

The late Ed McCaskey, who was married to Halas's daughter, Virginia, for many years, told a classic tale of his father-in-law's toughness.

"In 1960," McCaskey said, "we still used to charter a team train for the 200-mile trip to Green Bay, and Bears' fan clubs would hook a couple cars onto our train for the trip up and back."

The contingent would stay at the Northland Hotel, which, according to McCaskey, "was an experience in itself because Packer fans used to sneak in there all night long and set off fire alarms, stink bombs, and other stuff."

The outcome of this 1960 Bears' trip, which also happened to be legendary coach Vince Lombardi's second year in Green Bay, was not very successful. "The Packers hammered us pretty good, 41–13," said McCaskey. "We looked awful.

"So Coach [Halas] and I are walking down the railroad platform after the game to get on the train to go back to Chicago, and Coach is carrying a Bears' bag. I

THE BEARS: Chicago owner and coach George Halas with ends Walter Lamb and Jack Karwales, tackle Fred Davis, guard Chuck Drulis, and center Bulldog Turner, 1947.

HALAS VS. LOMBARDI: R-E-S-P-E-C-T

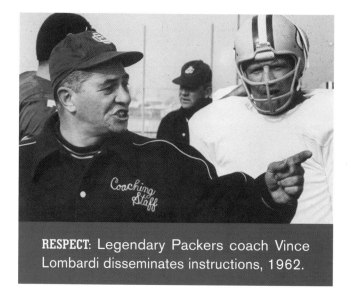

RESPECT: Legendary Packers coach Vince Lombardi disseminates instructions, 1962.

George Halas never even shook hands with Curly Lambeau in all the years the two men coached and plotted against each other in the NFL (see page 103). Given that, you might guess that Halas and Vince Lombardi, another Hall of Fame legend, would have had a hostile relationship during their nine years of match-ups (1959–1967).

Guess again.

"Lombardi and Halas were bitter rivals on the field," said Lee Remmel, "but great admirers of each other in every way."

Ed McCaskey said, "The only man I ever saw the Coach [Halas, his father-in-law] kiss was Lombardi. Coach loved that man and it broke his heart when Vince died of cancer [in September 1970]."

Lombardi won 13 of 18 clashes with Halas, including seven of the last eight. The Packers and Lombardi were NFL champions in 1961, 1962, 1965, 1966, and 1967. In 1963, when the Bears were kings of the NFL hill, they were 2–0 against Green Bay.

can still see this rough, tough Bears' fan rushing from between two cars in a red-and-black woolen shirt open halfway down his chest, with hair sticking out, and he snarls, 'Hey, Halas, why don't you quit?'

"And Coach drops the bag he was carrying right there and says, 'I'll show you why, you son of a bitch,' and he hauls off and hits the guy with a right to the chin. The guy was stunned—and he landed on his butt on the steps to a fans' train car. He had to be helped into the car by two of his pals. Coach was 65 at the time but he still was plenty tough."

Three years later, Halas's Bears were NFL champions.

THE RECENT PAST . . .

Halas died at age 88 in 1983, but he left behind Mike Ditka, his hell-hath-no-fury surrogate, as coach of the Bears. Chicago dominated the rivalry with Green Bay then—the Bears' talent was superior—but that didn't stop Ditka's blood from boiling when he saw green and gold.

From 1984–87, the Packers were coached by Forrest Gregg. In the 1960s, Ditka and Gregg had played against each other—Ditka as a tight end for the Bears, Gregg as an offensive tackle for the Packers. In 1971 they were teammates for a season in Dallas. Gregg was voted into the Hall of Fame in 1977; Ditka had to wait until 1988.

To put it mildly, the two men didn't like each other—for a lot of complex reasons. In a locker room speech in 1984, Gregg shouted, "You take care of the Bears, I'll take care of Ditka!"

STAT BOX

FIRST GAME

NOVEMBER 27, 1921 • STALEYS (BEARS) 20–PACKERS 0

LIFETIME HEAD-TO-HEAD RECORD

BEARS 85–PACKERS 78 (6 TIES)

DIVISION CHAMPIONSHIPS*

*SINCE 1970 MERGER

BEARS: 7

1984, 1985, 1986, 1987, 1988,

1990, 2001

PACKERS: 7

1972, 1995, 1996, 1997, 2002,

2003, 2004

NFL CHAMPIONSHIPS

BEARS: 9

1921, 1932, 1933, 1940, 1941,

1943, 1946, 1963, 1985

PACKERS: 12

1929, 1930, 1931, 1936, 1939,

1944, 1961, 1962, 1965, 1966,

1967, 1996

MOST LOPSIDED WIN

THE BEARS WHOMPED THE PACKERS 61–7 IN 1980

HOME FIELDS

BEARS: SOLDIER FIELD

PACKERS: LAMBEAU FIELD

HIGHLIGHT REEL
★★★★★

Lee Remmel Remembers

Having seen so many games in the rivalry, Lee Remmel, 81 and the Packers' official historian, smiles in pleasure when he is asked to name his most memorable Green Bay–Chicago games. His choices are offbeat and surprising.

1944

"In 1944, we took a 28–0 lead on the Bears but they came back to tie it at 28. Then we got two dramatic touchdowns in the fourth quarter to win 42–28."

1970

"In 1970, (quarterback) Bart Starr, near the end of his playing days and known for anything but his running skills, scored on a bootleg to beat the Bears 20–19."

1980

"In the 1980 preseason, we had looked as bad as any Packer team ever. We lost our last preseason game 38–0 and [coach] Bart Starr was beside himself. Yet we beat the Bears 12–6 in overtime in the opener when Chester Marcol, our kicker, ran a blocked kick in for a touchdown."

"I'LL TAKE CARE OF DITKA!": Bears coach Mike Ditka gets his game on, 1986.

In 1985 the Bears' epic 18–1 season, Ditka twice used mammoth defensive tackle Refrigerator Perry to score touchdowns in victories over Green Bay, leaving Gregg furious. Bears fullback Matt Suhey was knocked out after a play had been ruled dead in the second '85 game, and in 1986, Bears quarterback Jim McMahon was body-slammed after throwing an interception against Green Bay.

Ditka won seven of eight showdowns with Gregg but by an average of only eight points. To this day, the surest way to bring fire to Ditka's eyes is to mention Gregg and the Packers.

The two teams have played 169 times—168 in the regular season and once in the postseason (in 1941 they tied for first in the Western Division and had to have a playoff game; Chicago won).

A real rivalry is giving and taking, fighting and feuding. This is a Real Rivalry: the Bears have won 85 times, the Packers 78 times, and six games have ended in a draw.

Chicago has scored 2,880 points, Green Bay 2,762. The difference is less than one point per game.

And it is a rivalry that is a crazy-quilt of inter- and intra-rivalries, Tarzan Taylor's fist vs. Cub Buck's nose, Halas vs. a renegade Bears fan, and Ditka vs. Gregg being only a few.

For genuine long-running vitriol try Halas vs. Earl (Curly) Lambeau, who was a player-coach for the Packers' town team in 1919 at age 21. Lambeau coached the Packers for 31 seasons, through 1949, then coached the Chicago Cardinals and Washington Redskins for two seasons each. In all of those years that Lambeau faced Halas across the gridiron, the two men never shook hands on a football field. Off the field—in countless league meetings and in other dealings—their relationship was frosty at best.

"They would have done anything in the world to beat each other," Lee Remmel says. "Anything."

Willie Davis, the Packers' Hall of Fame defensive end in the 1960s, puts this annual home-and-home clash of old rivals in perspective.

"There have been great rivalries in American sport," Davis says, "but none with the fire-in-the-belly intensity as this one."

After all, what other rivalry can claim 52 Hall of Famers—28 Bears, 24 Packers?

—JOHN WIEBUSCH

John Wiebusch was the vice-president/editorial director of NFL Publishing and Creative for 32 years, the editor of 34 official Super Bowl programs, and the author or editor of dozens of books, including the classic *Lombardi*. He writes the "NFL Heroes and Legends" column for AOL.

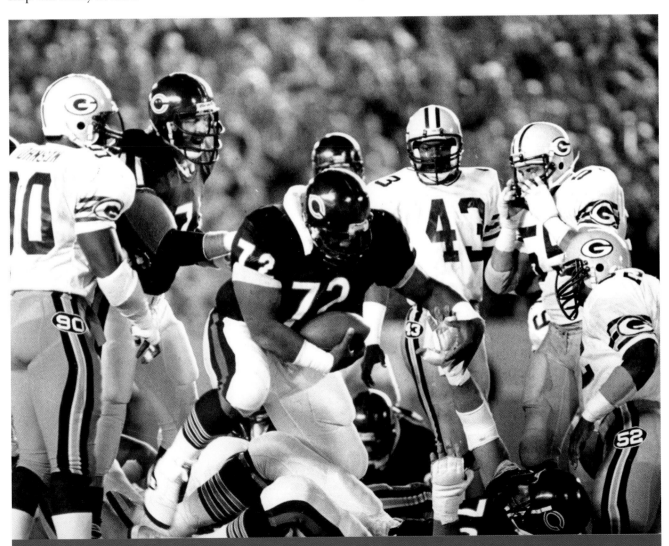

THE FRIDGE: Chicago Bears' William "Refrigerator" Perry (#72) surrounded by Packers, 1985. Though a defensive tackle, Perry was used to score touchdowns over Green Bay.

RICHARD PETTY *vs.* DAVID PEARSON

ARE GREAT ATHLETES' CAREERS DIMINISHED IF THEY DON'T HAVE RIVALS TO PUSH THEM? DO THEIR RECORDS SEEM lesser because they never had to rise to a challenge from equal gods? Is their legacy shrunk by the absence of worthy challengers?

In the high-speed world of NASCAR, stock-car racing's greatest champion had a foil worthy of his talents. For most of his long career, Richard "The King" Petty, NASCAR's greatest all-time champion, was pushed (or pulled) by David Pearson. Their head-to-head—or should we say, bumper-to-bumper—duels were legendary and made many races in the 1960s and 1970s battles for third place behind the famous pair.

Petty was raised in racing royalty. His father, Lee, was a three-time NASCAR champion in the 1950s and winner of the first Daytona 500 in 1959. Richard grew up around cars, working on his dad's crew until the old man let the kid take the wheel when he was 21. The younger Petty soon eclipsed his father's skills. "The first race I won, I was Lee's son. After that, I was Richard Petty," he said in 1967. In 1966 Petty became the first driver to win two Daytona 500s; he went on to win a record seven Daytonas. He won his first of seven NASCAR titles in 1964, a record that was later matched by the late Dale Earnhardt Sr.

While Petty had the door to NASCAR held open for him, Pearson had to knock it down. Working his way up through the dirt-track racing ranks, Pearson had a solid start when he made the top circuit in 1960, winning rookie of the year honors. But whereas Petty rocketed to the top, Pearson improved steadily. Even when he won his first overall championship in 1966, his seven race wins were dwarfed by Petty's 16, the most by a single driver in one season since Tim Flock's 18 in 1955.

After Pearson made the top circuit, the head-to-head rivalry between the two really caught the attention of racing fans. Throughout the 1960s and most of the 1970s, the two Carolinians (Petty from North, Pearson from South) were at the pinnacle of their sport. But though they often found themselves door-to-door on the final lap of races in front of millions, off the track they were very

TRAPPED BY A FOX

David Pearson is still regarded today as one of NASCAR's craftiest and smoothest drivers. A classic Silver Fox move came at the expense of his old rival Richard Petty in the 1974 Firecracker 400. On the final lap, with the lead in hand, Pearson suddenly slowed. Thinking No. 21 was having engine trouble, Petty raced ahead . . . right into Pearson's trap. The Silver Fox closed the gap to Petty's car with ease, waited for the right moment, and then roared around the King in a classic slingshot pass, using the draft created by Petty to gain a boost that took Pearson right through the finish line in first place.

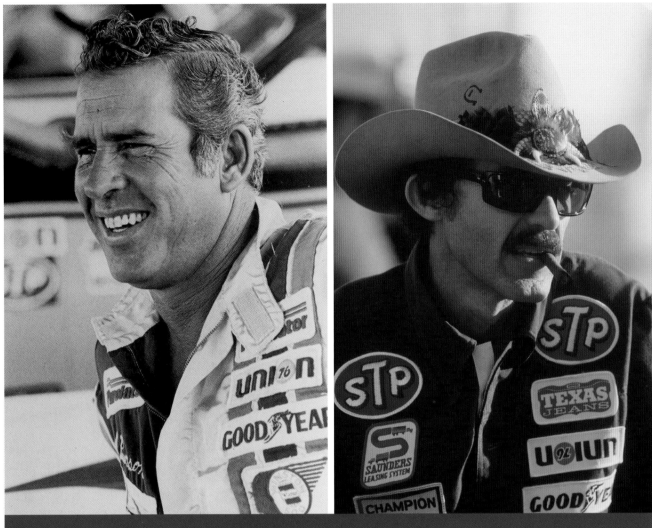

THE FOX AND THE KING: David Pearson (left) and Richard Petty. The duo dominated stock car racing in the late 1960s and 1970s.

different individuals. Pearson was Lou Gehrig to Petty's Babe Ruth; while Pearson embodied more the behind-the-scenes nuts and bolts of the sport, Petty represented the glad-handing, wide-smiled face of NASCAR.

Few athletes have dominated their sports as Petty did in the late 1960s and 1970s. At the same time, few three-time champions of a sport have ever been less celebrated than Pearson, the man they called the "Silver Fox." Pearson won NASCAR season titles in 1966, 1968, and 1969. Over the final two of those championship seasons, Pearson won 27 races and finished second 30 times. But in the midst of that, Petty won the title in 1967 in spectacular fashion, capturing a record 27 race victories in that year alone, including a stunning 10 in a row. Only real racing aficionados can tell you about Pearson's record; many sorts of sports fans can tell you about Petty's.

Between 1963 and 1977, the two finished first and second in an amazing 63 races. Pearson won 33 of those duels, with Petty winning the other 30. Looked at in that fashion, fully one-third of Pearson's career total of 105 wins came because he beat Richard Petty head-to-head to the checkered flag.

"When you lose to somebody better than you are, you don't mind it," Petty said graciously of Pearson in 2001.

Pearson's 105 race victories would be the most all-time in NASCAR if it were not for—surprise—Petty, whose total of 200 wins is perhaps the most insurmountable record in the sport. One record that Pearson does hold, even above the "King," is winning percentage. He won 105 of the 574 races he started, an 18.3 percent mark that is the best ever (for drivers starting at least 240 races).

Style-wise, the two men differed on the track as well.

HIGHLIGHT REEL

★ ★ ★ ★ ★

1964

Petty wins his first Daytona 500 and first NASCAR title.

1966

Pearson wins first NASCAR title.

1967

Petty wins 27 races and NASCAR title.

1968

Pearson wins NASCAR title.

1969

Pearson wins NASCAR title.

1971

Petty wins NASCAR title.

1972

Petty wins NASCAR title.

1974

Petty wins NASCAR title.

1975

Petty wins NASCAR title.

1976

Pearson wins Daytona 500 in duel with Petty.

1979

Petty wins NASCAR title.

1981

Petty wins his record seventh, and final, Daytona 500.

BYE-BYE: Richard Petty waves a greeting as he beats a very close David Pearson (top) in a 1975 race.

GREAT AMERICAN VICTORY: David Pearson displays his Daytona 500 trophy, 1976.

Whereas Petty was a hard-charging driver, roaring to the front, usually to stay, Pearson was craftier, using every trick in the book to get ahead. He'd use power and speed when he had to (he won 111 pole positions, second most all-time to Petty), guile when he could.

Every rivalry has a defining moment, an event that crystallizes what the rivalry meant and how it was perceived. Oddly, however, though Petty today owns the lion's share of acclaim and ended his career with more accomplishments, it was Pearson who came out ahead in their signature duel. It came during the 1976 Daytona 500, the "Great American Race" that kicks off each NASCAR season. Petty came into the race having already won it six times, including the two previous runnings. Pearson, for all of his success, had never won this big race, though he had won five other races at Daytona.

Amid the patriotic fervor that was America's Bicenntennial, several drivers held the lead for a time, but both Petty and Pearson were near the lead the whole way. With 12 laps to go, Petty moved into first place, and Pearson quickly fell in line behind him. The duo raced 1–2

until the final lap. Then the real fun started. As the two rocketed toward Turn 3, the end of the far straightaway at fabled Daytona, Pearson pulled out from behind and pulled off a perfect slingshot pass, zooming past Petty on the outside. The Fox had triggered the trap again, but this time, the King had a few tricks of his own.

As Pearson drifted a bit too high pulling through the turn, Petty dropped down toward the inside to take the lead, as the 250,000 hard-core fans screamed with excitement. This was NASCAR racing as good as it gets, the best two drivers nose-to-nose with the checkered flag just seconds away.

Suddenly, a nudge, a spin, then two spins, and both cars whacked in the wall, turned back, and slid down the track toward the grass infield, their front ends smashed and steam and smoke billowing. Petty had clipped Pearson's bumper as he tried to ride him off. Pearson had whanged right into the wall, followed by Petty.

Petty's red, white, and blue No. 43 Dodge came to rest, a battered, smoking heap. But Pearson's gold and white No. 21 Mercury, nearly as damaged, was still moving. The Silver Fox had focused on keeping his engine revving, even as he was heading toward the dirt. He managed to coax his dying car the few hundred yards to the finish line, the checkered flag waving over him as he cruised by at just over walking speed. Petty, as steamed as his car, could only watch helplessly.

Capping it off was the gracious response of Petty to the anger of his crew, who were looking for a fight after the drivers made it back to the pits. "If you want to blame somebody, blame me," he said, mollifying both teams.

The last-lap dramatics cemented the race as one of NASCAR's all-time best, and it was certainly the most memorable duel these two great drivers ever had. Petty might still be the all-time champ, the people's favorite, the record-setting public face of NASCAR, but on that day in Florida, the Silver Fox ruled supreme.

The rivalry that NASCAR fans still remember most (though some pairings have sparked some heat in recent years, none have come near surpassing these two legends) will be remembered for far more than one race. "What could be more beautiful," famous racing journalist Bill Robinson once wrote, "than Petty and Pearson, side by side, flat out and belly to the ground, racing toward a hurrying sundown."

—J.B.

STAT BOX

RICHARD PETTY

NICKNAME: THE "KING"

BORN: JULY 2, 1937, LEVEL CROSS, NORTH CAROLINA

NASCAR CAREER: 1958–1992

RACE WINS: 200 (MOST ALL-TIME)

NASCAR TITLES: (1964, 1967, 1971, 1972, 1974, 1975, 1979) 7*

*TIED FOR MOST ALL-TIME

INDUCTED INTO INTL. MOTORSPORTS HALL OF FAME: 1997

HEAD-TO-HEAD: IN 1–2 FINISHES WITH PEARSON, WON 30 OUT OF 63

POLE POSITIONS: 127

WINS FROM THE POLE: 61

TOP AVERAGE SPEED IN DAYTONA 500 WIN: 169.651 MPH IN 1981

DAVID PEARSON

NICKNAME: THE "SILVER FOX"

BORN: DECEMBER 22, 1934, WHITNEY, SOUTH CAROLINA

NASCAR CAREER: 1960–1986

RACE WINS: 105 (SECOND MOST ALL-TIME)

NASCAR TITLES: (1966, 1968, 1969) 3*

*TIED FOR THIRD-MOST ALL-TIME

INDUCTED INTO INTL. MOTORSPORTS HALL OF FAME: 1990

HEAD-TO-HEAD: IN 1–2 FINISHES WITH PETTY, WON 33 OUT OF 63

POLE POSITIONS: 113

WINS FROM THE POLE: 37

TOP AVERAGE SPEED IN DAYTONA 500 WIN: 152.181 MPH IN 1976

AFFIRMED *vs.* ALYDAR

ONE OF THE STRANGEST OBSERVATIONS ABOUT SPORTS RIVALRIES IS HOW ONE-SIDED SOME OF THEM CAN BE. THE Yankees dominated the Red Sox for most of a century. Bill Russell denied Wilt Chamberlain from celebrating a title for more than a decade. Bjorn Borg toyed with Jimmy Connors for years. And in 1977 and 1978, you could bet on thoroughbred standout Affirmed to beat Alydar when it counted. Yet it wasn't just Affirmed's consistent wins that built the rivalry; it was the heart-stopping way in which he won, in split-second finishes ahead of archrival Alydar. The competition between Affirmed and Alydar was so intense and so close it defied explanation.

"Whatever it is that these two horses have cannot be bought or manufactured," said the legendary trainer Woody Stephens. "It's the greatest act horse racing has ever had."

Horse racing history has seldom seen two three-year-olds as good as Affirmed and Alydar in the same season. They were animals, yet their appeal went beyond racing and touched people in a way that few human athletes are capable of. Even people who did not normally follow horse racing came to know the competitors' pedigrees. Alydar was Kentucky-bred, raised on the famous Calumet Farm by owner John Veitch, who brought aboard veteran jockey Jorge Velasquez. Affirmed, on the other hand, was Florida-bred, out of Harbor View Farm and trained by Laz Barrera. The difference-maker was Affirmed's rider, Steve Cauthen. Standing barely taller than five feet and weighing 95 pounds, they called him the "Kid"—and not just in reference to his size. It was just two years since he rode his first race at the tender age of 16, aboard a 136-to-1 longshot named King of Swat that finished next-to-last. Little did he know that a year later he would receive the Eclipse Award of Merit as the sport's most outstanding jockey and that the following year he would be at Churchill Downs to race in the Kentucky Derby.

As a young boy Cauthen dreamed of one day winning the Derby. He grew up on a horse farm in Walton, Kentucky, straddling a hay bale and whipping an imaginary colt to victory. At age nine he visited the Downs with a longtime friend of the family who knew the owner of the winning horse and afterwards gave Cauthen a rose from the winner's traditional blanket of roses. The dream of earning his own roses at the famous racetrack burned brightly, and Cauthen dedicated himself to becoming a top jockey.

In 1977 Cauthen, then only 17, was an apprentice jockey when he outdistanced the competition, leading the entire country in races and money won. The media hailed him as a prodigy, a marvel, a comet, and a phenomenon, yet Cauthen remained grounded. The night before the 1978 Kentucky Derby he slept on the floor in the hotel room he shared with his parents and two brothers.

Cauthen rode with a great, natural sense of balance, what jockeys call "seat." In fact, his parents have a home

"IT'S THE GREATEST ACT HORSE RACING HAS EVER HAD" —LEGENDARY TRAINER WOODY STEPHENS

BY A NOSE: Affirmed and jockey Steve Cauthen (right) gain a short lead at the 1978 Belmont Stakes, on the way to clinching Affirmed's Triple Crown win.

video in which a two-year-old Cauthen rides a pony by himself. So unique was Cauthen's posture, even without the flamingo pink and black silk uniform of Harbor View Farm, he could easily be picked out among the other jockeys in a pack. Cauthen rode with his head very still and his spine perfectly parallel to the ground. Veteran stable grooms were fond of saying that you could place a drink on Cauthen's back in the starting gate and not spill a drop before the finish line.

The Triple Crown—the attainment of wins in the three most vaunted races—is horse racing's greatest prize, and heading into the first of 1978's racing series, the Kentucky Derby, both horses' camps felt their mount had a shot at the elusive prize. Alydar had won the 1977 Champagne Stakes at Belmont Park that usually determines the best two-year-old in the country, but the second-place horse in that race, Affirmed, who had beaten Alydar

three of the five times they had met, won the surprise vote, with Alydar a close second. Then Alydar won the Florida Derby in the fastest time in 30 years and had to be looked at as the horse to beat in the upcoming Triple Crown. The racing world was abuzz about the match-up, but the wider world had heard, for the most part, only of Cauthen. That would soon change.

On the morning of the Derby, Cauthen and Barrera plotted strategy. They knew the main horse to beat was indeed Alydar, a come-from-behind runner and the Derby favorite. All they wanted was a nice, clean break at the start and then it would be Cauthen's decision when to take off. The race happened exactly the way they predicted. Once the starting gate opened Alydar had trouble gaining traction on the dirt and fell far behind the leaders. Cauthen nimbly kept Affirmed within striking distance until the mile, then clicked his heels and the chestnut colt bolted

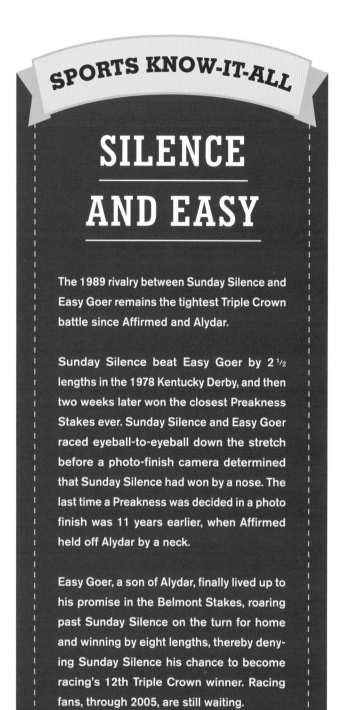

SILENCE
AND EASY

The 1989 rivalry between Sunday Silence and Easy Goer remains the tightest Triple Crown battle since Affirmed and Alydar.

Sunday Silence beat Easy Goer by 2½ lengths in the 1978 Kentucky Derby, and then two weeks later won the closest Preakness Stakes ever. Sunday Silence and Easy Goer raced eyeball-to-eyeball down the stretch before a photo-finish camera determined that Sunday Silence had won by a nose. The last time a Preakness was decided in a photo finish was 11 years earlier, when Affirmed held off Alydar by a neck.

Easy Goer, a son of Alydar, finally lived up to his promise in the Belmont Stakes, roaring past Sunday Silence on the turn for home and winning by eight lengths, thereby denying Sunday Silence his chance to become racing's 12th Triple Crown winner. Racing fans, through 2005, are still waiting.

---

in the Triple Crown, was another sizzling stride-for-stride duel between the two horses, with never more than half a length separating them as they rumbled around the $1\frac{3}{16}$ mile oval course. Riding with clocklike precision, Cauthen never panicked, and Alydar, true to the script, was again the bridesmaid. Affirmed won the Preakness by a neck because he dug in when things got toughest and refused to be overtaken. Trackside observers noted that if Affirmed was in front at the top of the stretch, you could put your binoculars down because no horse could catch him. And Cauthen was a master at directing a horse to the front of the field and then bringing him home.

With the Preakness victory Cauthen had fully captivated the racing public. It had been three years since the legendary Secretariat had retired, and racing was in a lull and in need of a superstar. Cauthen's pursuit of the Triple Crown made him the sport's most recognizable figure, drawing large crowds and television ratings. The acclaim spread to the general public, and the young rider landed on the covers of *TIME*, *Newsweek*, and *Sports Illustrated* in the same week, an impressive trifecta. Now all that stood between Affirmed and immortality was the Belmont Stakes, the grueling mile-and-a-half "test of the champion." It proved to be the most dramatic Belmont in history. This time Alydar shed his blinkers—devices placed on some race horses to restrict their peripheral vision—and attacked much earlier than in either the Derby or the Preakness.

"I knew that Alydar would come up [quicker] and we would fight it out," said Cauthen. "I didn't think we'd have to fight it out for a mile, but with Affirmed and Alydar it always seems to turn out that they fight for every inch."

An inch was about all that separated the horses as they ran head to head around the track. The two horses were so close together that they looked like one animal. Sweeping around the final turn, there was little daylight between them. As they raced furiously down the stretch, Alydar momentarily seemed to stick his nose in front, but then Cauthen switched the stick from his right hand and did something he had never done before—he whipped Affirmed with his left hand, striking the horse's left flank nine times. The chestnut colt responded quickly and pushed his nose back in front. Then they were dead even again with ten yards to go. As they crossed the finish line Affirmed's head was ever-so-slightly in front, but it took a photo-finish camera to confirm it for the wildly cheering

to a two-length lead. At the top of the stretch Velasquez led Alydar on a furious charge, but it came too late and 1½ lengths too short. Cauthen's Derby dream had come true, and horse racing's greatest rivalry was established.

Two weeks after the Derby, a crowd of 81,261, the largest ever to watch a sporting event in Maryland, came out to see the second act of Affirmed against Alydar in the Preakness Stakes at Pimlico Race Track in Baltimore. They were not disappointed. The Preakness, the second "jewel"

BY A LENGTH AND A HALF: Affirmed and Cauthen (right) cross the finish line to win the Kentucky Derby ahead of Alydar and jockey Jorge Velasquez, 1978.

EQUINE ROYALTY: Affirmed poses with trainer Laz Barrera. Affirmed was only the 11th horse to win the Triple Crown. None have won it since.

crowd of 65,417 and a television audience of millions. But Cauthen knew he had won, for he stood up in the saddle a few yards past the finish and waved his left hand high in the air.

"Part of what made me feel so good about the Belmont was we were put under pressure the whole way, and we didn't crack," said Cauthen, at age 18 the youngest jockey in history to win the Triple Crown. "The horse and I stood up under the toughest pressure you can ever come under. It was a great feeling—and a relief to get past the wire."

Affirmed became the 11th horse to achieve the Triple Crown, and, through 2005, the last horse to do so. No horse ever worked harder for it or deserved it more. Affirmed's total margin in the three races was fewer than two lengths. Affirmed had beaten Alydar in the Kentucky Derby by a length and a half, in the Preakness by a neck, and in the Belmont by a nose. Never has a Triple Crown sweep been sealed by such a narrow margin.

Back at his stall after the Belmont, Alydar's trainer John Veitch was in a somber and reflective mood. "Do I think that Affirmed has broken Alydar's heart? No. Not with a horse like Alydar. He's just too good. There isn't a thing in the world for Alydar to be ashamed of."

Never before had two horses fought each other so frequently in a rivalry that produced such close decisions. It is a pity that Alydar has the distinction to be remembered as the only horse to finish second in all three Triple Crown races to a Triple Crown winner. To be sure, Alydar would have been a champion in almost any other year. But timing is everything. Said Veitch, the vanquished trainer but ever the sportsman: "People in the horse business might say, 'What a shame it is that Affirmed and Alydar came along in the same year because one must win and the other must lose.' I won't say that because it's silly. The two are a marvelous thing for racing."

—D.F.

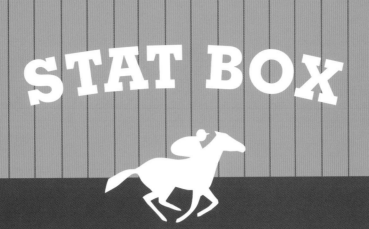

STAT BOX

AFFIRMED

BORN: FEBRUARY 21, 1975

LIFETIME RECORD: 22 VICTORIES IN 29 RACES

LIFETIME PURSE WINNINGS: $2,393,818

YEARS RACED: 1977-1979

1977: 9 STARTS, 7 WINS, 2 PLACES

• KEY VICTORIES: YOUTHFUL STAKES, HOPEFUL STAKES,
   BELMONT FUTURITY

1978: 11 STARTS, 8 WINS, 2 PLACES

• KEY VICTORIES: TRIPLE CROWN

1979: 9 STARTS, 7 WINS, 2 PLACES

• KEY VICTORIES: HOLLYWOOD GOLD CUP, SANTA ANITA HANDICAP,
   WOODWARD STAKES, JOCKEY CLUB GOLD CLUB

ALYDAR

BORN: MARCH 23, 1975

LIFETIME RECORD: 14 VICTORIES IN 26 RACES

LIFETIME PURSE WINNINGS: $957,195

YEARS RACED: 1977-1979

1977: 10 STARTS, 5 WINS, 4 PLACES

• KEY VICTORIES: SAPLING, GRADE 1 CHAMPAGNE STAKES

1978: 10 STARTS, 7 WINS, 3 PLACES

• KEY VICTORIES: BLUE GRASS STAKES, FLAMINGO STAKES,
   FLORIDA DERBY, ARLINGTON CLASSIC, WHITNEY, TRAVERS

1979: 6 STARTS, 2 WINS, 3 PLACES

• KEY VICTORIES: NASSAU COUNTY HANDICAP

LAKERS *vs.* CELTICS

I N NO OTHER PRO SPORT HAVE TWO TEAMS SO DOMINATED FOR SUCH A LONG PERIOD OF TIME. THE NBA HAS CROWNED an annual champion 58 times (through 2005) since its first official season in 1948; the Lakers and Celtics have combined to win an astonishing 30 of them. By comparison, the Yankees have won 26 World Series, but that's less than a quarter of all the baseball titles. The Lakers and Celtics own 52 percent of all the NBA titles.

On ten occasions, they faced each other in the NBA Finals, making it the most-seen match-up in that championship series.

The Lakers were the first to dominate, winning five NBA titles while based in Minneapolis in the 1940s and 1950s (they moved to L.A. in 1960). The Celtics won their first title in 1956. None of those wins came at the direct expense of the other team, however, and the rivalry between the two really began when the Celts, led by the remarkable point guard Bob Cousy, defeated Minneapolis in 1959 to win the first of their all-time record eight consecutive championships. It's a record unmatched in major pro sports—and the losers in six of those final series were the Lakers.

The Lakers boasted some of the finest players in basketball history: forward Elgin Baylor and guard Jerry West (such a model of basketball excellence that it is his silhouette modeled on the NBA logo) among them. But the Celtics had some stars of their own, in the form of Cousy, the mold out of whom all future point guards would be made, and center Bill Russell, the dominant defensive force in the game. From Russell's arrival in 1957 to his retirement in 1969, the Celtics won 11 championships. Russell's defensive skills and rebounding expertise both add to his legacy, but in the end, it's his pile of championship rings that makes the lasting impression.

The 1962 Finals match-up between the two teams was the first of six such rivalry match-ups in the 1960s . . . all won by Boston. The '62 series remains one of the all-time best. The teams split the first two games, played in the legendary Boston Garden. In Game Three, West stole an inbounds pass and made a lay-up at the buzzer to steal the win. But Boston came back to win the next game. In Game Five, Baylor set an NBA Finals record with 61 points in a dominant Lakers' win. Yet back in L.A. for Game Six, Boston won again on its rival's home court. Game Seven was a classic, the only overtime final game ever played to determine the NBA champ. Russell grabbed a record 40 rebounds, the Lakers' Frank Selvy missed a last-second shot that could have won it in regulation, and the Celtics triumphed, 110–107. They would be taken to a Game Seven in the Finals only twice more in the next six years.

The end of the rivalry's first era came after the 1969 season, when Russell led the Celts to his last title, going up for the first time in the finals against his own archrival Wilt Chamberlain. The mighty "Stilt" had joined the

GAME SEVEN WAS A CLASSIC, THE ONLY OVERTIME FINAL GAME EVER PLAYED TO DETERMINE THE NBA CHAMP.

LAKER SANDWICH: Celtics' Bob Cousy breaks through Minnesota Lakers' James Raxon (left) and Bob Leonard, 1957.

ARCHRIVAL AND NEMESIS: Celtics star Bill Russell (#6) shoots as the Lakers' Wilt Chamberlain (#13) goes up for the block in the 1969 playoffs. The Celts won the series, which was Russell's last.

RUSSELL VS. CHAMBERLAIN

In 1959, a giant man-child from Kansas arrived in the NBA and began to do things no one had ever seen a man of his size (7'1") do. Wilt Chamberlain became the first player to win the rookie of the year award and the MVP trophy in the same season. He set single-game and season records for rebounds. Three years later, he would become the only player ever to score 100 points in a game. He averaged more than 50 points per game over an entire season (1961–1962). Wilt "The Stilt" remade how basketball was played, combining height, power, and dexterity as none before.

But he was not the most successful player of his era. Instead, to Wilt's eternal frustration, Bill Russell won and won and won. Chamberlain routinely outscored Russell, but also often watched as Russell and his Celtics went home with the victory. Russell also earned the majority of the positive accolades tossed around by writers and fans. "Their favorite, even after I came into the league, was Bill Russell," Chamberlain wrote in his 1973 book *Wilt*, after listing numerous stats proving his dominance. "Why? I've asked myself that question a thousand times, and I'm not very happy with any of the answers."

It's a debate that will continue whenever hoops fans reminisce, and, like many such important questions, it's one without a final answer.

Lakers after leading Philly to the title in 1967, breaking the Celtics' reign. Russell wanted one more title, and Chamberlain ached to defeat his nemesis. It was Russell who received his wish, as the Celtics squeaked out a two-point win in a dramatic Game Seven on the Lakers' Fabulous Forum home court. Russell retired after the game, and the team that was basketball's most dominant of all time faded away.

Chamberlain's Lakers won a title in 1972, but didn't beat the Celtics to earn it. The Celts won in 1974 and 1976, but without having to do the rivalry dance.

The star-studded history between the teams, one-sided though it was, helped fuel the rebirth of the rivalry in the 1980s. Again, each team was led by remarkable players: the Lakers by Earvin "Magic" Johnson, perhaps the finest all-around point guard in league history, and Kareem Abdul-Jabbar, the NBA's all-time leading scorer; the Celtics by Larry Bird, a dead-eye shooter and wizardly passer, and the tall-tree, front-court duo of Robert Parrish and Kevin McHale.

Magic joined the Lakers in 1979 and led them to an NBA title as a rookie. Bird carried the Celts to a title in 1980. Game on!

From 1979 to 1988, the Lakers or Celtics won every NBA title except one (Philadelphia won in 1983). Three times the two teams had to play each other for the league's ultimate prize, awakening echoes of the 1960s match-ups but with a modern flair.

"The most fun I had playing basketball was playing against the Lakers," Bird said. "When a Celtic gets beat by a Laker, you get this sickness in your gut, the worst feeling you could ever have."

"Hate is a heavy word, but yeah, you hated them," Johnson said. He added, in his autobiography *My Life*, "When we played the Celtics, I was as emotionally high as I could possibly be."

So when the reinvented teams met for the title for the first time in 1984, sports fans rejoiced at the chance to see the pair head-to-head. The players didn't disappoint.

That year, Bird won the league MVP, dazzling fans with his passing game and demonstrating nightly one of the best shooting touches seen in decades. Magic was, well, magic, and kept up the "Showtime" style of ball he had helped start in glitzy L.A.

Back-and-forth action led to a 2–2 tie by Game Five. A hard foul in Game Four by Kevin McHale on the

A MAGIC MOMENT: Magic Johnson goes for a layup in a game against the Celtics, 1983.

Lakers' Kurt Rambis nearly started a fight. Johnson admitted later that the Celtics had "intimidated us with their physical game . . . we just rolled over." The Celtics won Game Five in the Boston Garden. The ancient Garden was not exactly a garden spot, and the 97-degree temperatures outside made the arena a sweat lodge for players and fans alike. "It was like running in mud," said Abdul-Jabbar. Game Six was back in L.A. and the Lakers evened the series. Back to Beantown for the deciding Game Seven. A Lakers team had never clinched a title over a Boston team in NBA history, and certainly not in the venerable "Gahden," and it was no different this night. A gaffe by Johnson at the end helped seal the Lakers' fate and the first Magic-Bird battle went to the Hick from French Lick (Bird's Indiana hometown). Bird became only the fourth player ever to be named both the regular-season and Finals MVP.

The next year, the roles were reversed, and it was Magic who helped hoist the trophy after the Lakers won in six games. The Lakers rebounded from a stunning Game One defeat, losing 148–114 in a game dubbed the Memorial Day Massacre.

"That game was a blessing in disguise," said Lakers coach Pat Riley. "It strengthened the fiber of the team."

Taking a 3–2 lead with a Game Five win in Los Angeles, the Lakers knew they had to return to Boston and win at least one game to claim the title, something no Lakers team had ever done. Led by Abdul-Jabbar and Magic, along with scoring forward James Worthy and defensive ace Michael Cooper, they did it, winning that final game 111–100.

"The sweetest sound I ever heard," wrote Magic, "was the silence in Boston Garden after we took a commanding lead in Game Six in 1985." The curse of the Garden ended; the Lakers were champs.

The "rubber game" of their trio of title tilts came in 1987, and the Lakers again carried home the crown. Again, the focus was almost entirely on Bird vs. Magic, as it had been in hoops since their 1979 NCAA title-game match-up (see box on page 122). In the end, though, it was Magic who put the capper on this legendary rivalry between both superstars and superteams. His baby hook over Parish and McHale with two seconds left clinched Game Four and helped send the Lakers to a six-game victory.

Age and time have mellowed the pair, of course, and

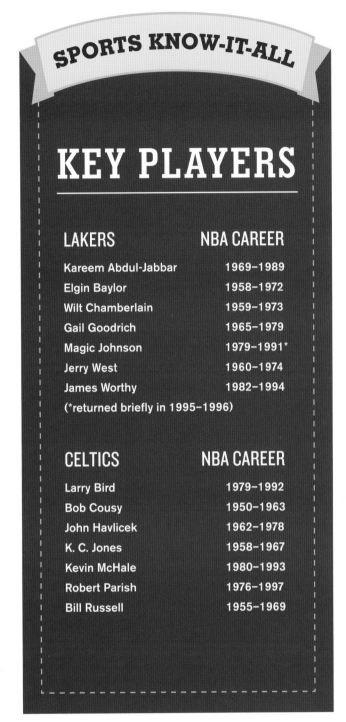

SPORTS KNOW-IT-ALL
KEY PLAYERS

LAKERS	NBA CAREER
Kareem Abdul-Jabbar	1969–1989
Elgin Baylor	1958–1972
Wilt Chamberlain	1959–1973
Gail Goodrich	1965–1979
Magic Johnson	1979–1991*
Jerry West	1960–1974
James Worthy	1982–1994

(*returned briefly in 1995–1996)

CELTICS	NBA CAREER
Larry Bird	1979–1992
Bob Cousy	1950–1963
John Havlicek	1962–1978
K. C. Jones	1958–1967
Kevin McHale	1980–1993
Robert Parish	1976–1997
Bill Russell	1955–1969

they moved on. Bird even presented Johnson when he was enshrined into the Basketball Hall of Fame in 2002. But retirement couldn't completely quell that powerful urge to compete that helped them gain so much success. "Even today," Johnson said at the event in Springfield, Massachussetts, "if these people weren't here, we'd be playing HORSE right now. We'd be going at each other and both of us would want to win. We're still two crazy, possessed guys, even at our age."

While the two players became old friends, the fabled

BIRD VS.
MAGIC

Lakers–Celtics is the rare rivalry that spawned not one, but two, equally classic individual rivalries. First came Russell and Chamberlain; then Magic and Bird.

Magic Johnson and Larry Bird first met each other on the basketball court when Magic's run-and-gun Michigan State team faced Bird's one-man-show Indiana State squad for the 1979 NCAA title. Magic won that night, and the rivalry was on.

After Magic led the Lakers to a surprising 1980 NBA title, Bird shot the lights out of the place while leading Boston to the 1981 championship. For the next decade, their match-ups on the court were the centerpiece of the sport.

Magic on Bird (from *My Life*, Johnson's 1993 autobiography): "Larry was the only player I feared. I felt confident that the Lakers could beat any team in the league, and we usually did. But when we played the Celtics, no lead was safe while Larry was on the floor. When you beat Larry Bird, you knew you had beaten the best."

Bird on Magic: "He played the game like I always wanted to play the game. To be able to control the ball and make plays. That's how I always envisioned a basketball player. I envision a player coming out and making things happen." That description, of course, applies equally to both rivals.

DEAD-EYE SHOOTER: Larry Bird shoots against the Lakers at the Boston Garden, 1980.

rivalry between these two great hardwood franchises faded with time. Magic Johnson retired first, in 1991, after being diagnosed as HIV-positive. He made some short returns, but left for good after the 1996 season. Bird retired in 1992. Wilt Chamberlain died in 1999, still worrying about whether everyone thought Bill Russell was better than him. The Lakers did rise again to the top of the NBA charts, winning three straight championships from 1999–2002, but they didn't once have to beat the Celtics in those Finals. The Celtics haven't been in the Finals since 1987, the Lakers moved out of the Fabulous Forum in 1999, and the Boston Garden closed down in 1995.

The teams still play during the regular season a couple of times, but the only rivalry can be found in the memories of fans and players as they look up at the retired jerseys that hang by the dozen over each team's court. The stars look down, and the fans remember.

—J.B.

STAT BOX

FIRST GAME

NOVEMBER 9, 1948 • CELTICS 77–LAKERS 55

LIFETIME HEAD-TO-HEAD RECORD

CELTICS 180–LAKERS 137

NBA CHAMPIONSHIPS

CELTICS: 16

1956–1957, 1958–1959, 1959–1960, 1960–1961, 1961–1962, 1962–1963, 1963–1964, 1964–1965, 1965–1966, 1967–1968, 1968–1969, 1973–1974, 1975–1976, 1980–1981, 1983–1984, 1985–1986

LAKERS: 14

1948–1949, 1949–1950, 1951–1952, 1952–1953, 1953–1954, 1971–1972, 1979–1980, 1981–1982, 1984–1985, 1986–1987, 1987–1988, 1999–2000 2000–2001, 2001–2002

NBA FINALS GAME 7's

1983–1984 SEASON: BOSTON WINS 111–102 IN BOSTON

1968–1969 SEASON: BOSTON WINS 108–106 IN LOS ANGELES

1965–1966 SEASON: BOSTON WINS 95–93 IN BOSTON

1961–1962 SEASON: BOSTON WINS 110–107 IN OVERTIME IN BOSTON

CHRIS EVERT *vs.*
MARTINA NAVRATILOVA

THE RELATIVELY RECENT ADVENT OF WOMEN'S SPORTS ON THE MAJOR WORLD SCENE (COMPARED TO, FOR INSTANCE, the 100-plus-year rivalry of the Harvard and Yale football teams) means that there is a smaller universe to draw from when looking at great rivalries. However, in any discussion of rivalries, male or female, one deserves inclusion among the most formidable ever. For more than 15 years, two women, as different as night and day, east and west, calm and storm, dominated their sport of tennis, achieving greatness both in spite of and with the help of the other. The 15-year rivalry between them also elevated women's tennis, partly for their stunning abilities and success, but also because they were a study in contrasts: a Czech expatriate who became open about her lesbianism against the American "girl next door."

The stats alone are staggering. Chris Evert and Martina Navratilova played in the women's singles finals of 22 Grand Slam tennis tournaments. Navratilova won 14 of those match-ups, including seven of nine Wimbledon finals and three of four U.S. Open championship matches. But Evert was certainly no second fiddle, setting a career record for all-time singles victories (a record topped after Evert's retirement by none other than . . . Navratilova. Evert won 157 singles titles in her career; Navratilova claimed 167).

They met for the first time in Akron, Ohio, on March 22, 1973, with Evert winning 7–6, 6–3. Already known for the steady baseline strokes and steely attitude that would remain her trademark, Evert dominated the early years of the rivalry, winning 21 of the first 25 matches they played, though Navratilova later firmly turned the tide. In their 80 head-to-head matches over all, Navratilova prevailed, 43–37.

Fittingly, Evert won her career's first important tourna-ment by defeating Navratilova 6–3, 6–3, in the women's singles final of the 1974 Italian Open. Navratilova was also playing for the first time on the big stage, and from the start she seemed unnerved by the attention. Clearly outclassed by Evert's consistent barrage of laser-beam passing shots that found the corners of the court, Navratilova succumbed in only 80 minutes. The turning point came when Evert broke in the seventh game of the second set to turn a 3–3 tie into a 6–3 victory. In that seventh game each player conceded the other a point after two poor calls by a line judge, a display of sportsmanship that would always mark their mutual respect and admiration for one another.

For two people so firmly linked together throughout tennis history, they were almost complete opposites—both in their playing styles and in their personalities. The blonde Evert was frilly and feminine, cutting a graceful figure with a calculating style of play. The more solidly built Navratilova acted much tougher and played with all-out aggression. Evert, cool and conservative, earned the nickname the "Ice Princess." Navratilova was emotional and volatile. Evert was not the least bit controversial. Navratilova became, later in her career, an activist at the forefront of the gay-rights movement. Evert appeared robotic and mechanical. Navratilova looked like the world was out to get her. And yet, somehow, these two disparate beings found a common ground on and off the court. What began as an on-court rivalry became a friendship formed by shared experience. Who else to appreciate the pressures and responsibilities of life at the top of a sport better? They never became "best buddies," but respect and maturity created a friendship.

"Her fans appreciated what she stood for and my

FRIENDS AND FOES: Chris Evert, right, and Martina Navratilova embrace after Navratilova wins the Wimbledon tennis championship, 1978.

TWO FOR THE SHOW: The doubles team of Evert and Navratilova present a formidable challenge to their opposition at Wimbledon, 1976.

fans appreciated what I stood for," Evert said. As the new president of the Women's Tennis Association, Evert was a consensus builder, and in the days of a friendlier locker room, the two young players talked often. "It was about how we looked, how we acted, our style, where we came from," Evert said. She quickly came to understand and appreciate Navratilova's sensitive personality. The two young players even joined up to become doubles partners. They won the 1975 French Open and 1976 Wimbledon doubles championships together. It's hard to imagine a more potent pairing: Evert, the master of the baseline strategy teamed with Navratilova, the best serve-and-volleyer the women's game has ever known.

Evert became the first of the pair to win a Grand Slam singles title, winning the 1974 French Open and beginning an incredible achievement of capturing at least one Grand Slam singles title in each of the next 13 years. The next year Evert won her first U.S. Open, but it was Navratilova who gained the headlines. After losing in straight sets to Evert in the semifinal match,

Navratilova, 18, asked for—and received—political asylum in the United States. Unlike the stereotypical Soviet bloc athlete of the time, Navratilova was (and remains) an exuberant personality given to gesturing, screaming, and glaring during matches. Self-described as a free-spirited, independent-thinking individual, Navratilova's tastes ranged from a love of American food to outlandish clothing. During that U.S. Open, she wore a garish, brightly colored floral print outfit which she described as "my favorite dress because it's like my personality—wild!" Several valid reasons accompanied Navratilova's request for a change in residency, including the fact that Czechoslovakia allowed its players to keep only a percentage of their earnings. Another possible reason for her defection was the opportunity for large-scale commercial endorsements in America. But mostly it was a matter of moral principles. Said Navratilova: "I've always had this outrage against being told how to live, what to say, how to act, what to do, when to do it."

Navratilova was 21 when she won the first of her

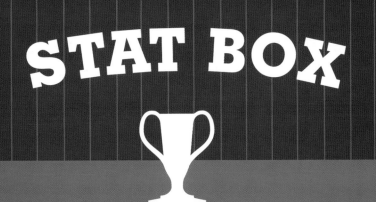

STAT BOX

FIRST MEETING

MARCH 22, 1973 • EVERT WON 7–6, 6–3

LIFETIME HEAD-TO-HEAD RECORD

NAVRATILOVA 43–EVERT 37

CHRIS EVERT

BORN: DECEMBER 21, 1954, FORT LAUDERDALE, FLORIDA

ALL-TIME SINGLES TOURNAMENT VICTORIES: 157

GRAND SLAM CHAMPIONSHIPS: 18

FRENCH OPEN: 1974, 1975, 1979, 1980, 1983, 1985, 1986

WIMBLEDON: 1974, 1976, 1981

U.S. OPEN: 1975, 1976, 1977, 1978, 1980, 1982

AUSTRALIAN OPEN: 1982, 1984

MARTINA NAVRATILOVA

BORN: OCTOBER 18, 1956, PRAGUE, CZECHOSLOVAKIA

ALL-TIME SINGLES TOURNAMENT VICTORIES: 167

GRAND SLAM CHAMPIONSHIPS: 18

FRENCH OPEN: 1982, 1984

WIMBLEDON: 1978, 1979, 1982, 1983, 1984, 1985, 1986, 1987, 1990

U.S. OPEN: 1983, 1984, 1986, 1987

AUSTRALIAN OPEN: 1981, 1983, 1985

HIGHLIGHT REEL
★ ★ ★ ★ ★

March 22, 1973
First meeting.

1978
Navratilova's first Wimbleton title.

1983
Navratilova beats Evert at the U.S. Open for first time.

1985
Evert wins their dramatic French Open battle.

1989
Evert retires.

1992
Navratilova breaks Evert's singles title record.

7–5 to win her first major singles title. Navratilova wept and said she was sad that her parents were not there. She had not seen them since she defected. Her tears were a show of a type of emotion tennis fans were not accustomed to seeing from the exuberant Czech; though they'd seen many emotions come pouring out of Navratilova, she had never seemed to show a tender side.

In 1981 Navratilova started serious weight training and developed a workout regimen that far surpassed that of her female competitors. She dropped 22 pounds through diet and exercise, morphing from her previous slightly rounded physique to show other players on the tour that women athletes could have muscles, too.

Navratilova had won titles in England, Australia, and France, but never the championship of her adopted country, the U.S. Open. That tournament was still Evert's domain, for she had captured six U.S. titles by that time. In 1983 Navratilova beat Evert 6–1, 6–3 to finally win her first major American title. Following her defection to America and her new workout routines, the scales of dominance were clearly tipping toward Navratilova. She had whipped Evert for the 13th time in a row and won her second consecutive U.S. Open title in three tough sets, in September 1984. Much of Evert's frustration during this dominant Navratilova period was that Evert was playing consistently well enough to make the finals, only to be beaten by Navratilova over and over again.

Evert let a marvelous opportunity to finally beat Navratilova slip through her fingers in the 1984 U.S. Open final. After winning the first set, Evert owned the capacity crowd at the stadium court of the National Tennis Center in Flushing Meadow, Queens, while Navratilova paced around the court with a look of disdain on her face, as if she had no idea why the crowd would cheer her opponent. Evert noted afterwards that the crowd was "deafening" for her, but in the end, the support didn't bring her game up enough. Navratilova would later say it was "the hardest thing I've ever been through—all those people wanting me to lose." Navratilova edged Evert in three tough sets 4–6, 6–4, 6–4 and won her sixth consecutive Grand Slam title, following up on a 1983 season in which she had won Wimbledon, the U.S. Open, and the Australian (then held in December).

After the '84 U.S. Open Evert said, "Sometimes I think it's me, that I can't finish out the match. Then I realize most of it's Martina. It's just not enough to play a good

record nine Wimbledon titles, in 1978. Grass was clearly her best surface, perfect for her style of play. But when Navratilova reached the final, she wondered if her parents were even aware of her accomplishment. "I'm not sure how they'll find out," she said after winning the semifinal match. "Since I defected three years ago there hasn't been a word about me in the Czech newspapers. Tomorrow they will probably say that Chris Evert is playing somebody in the Wimbledon finals. My parents will figure it out, or they will hear it on Voice of America." As it turned out, word indeed had reached her parents Miroslav and Jana, and they drove 80 miles from Prague to the West German border to watch the telecast of the match on a German television station. What they witnessed was their daughter twice coming back from behind to beat Evert 2–6, 6–4,

PRE-BATTLE: Evert and Navratilova pose for the press before a Virginia Slims Series tournament match, 1980.

match against her anymore." With that win in '84, Navratilova had tied Evert's record 55-match winning streak, which Navratilova would extend to an unprecedented 74 consecutive matches. It is by far the longest winning streak, male or female, in tennis history.

Evert was determined to return to the mountaintop of women's tennis and also went into the gym to get her body fit. She set her sights on the 1985 French Open, where the slower clay of the Roland Garros courts favored a player with sound ground strokes. Evert had beaten Navratilova only once in their last 16 matches when the two faced off in the French Open final. In this seesaw match, Navratilova had game points in each of the first three games but fell behind 0–3. She won the next three games, but then Evert won the next

three and the first set. Navratilova's serve came alive, and she won the second set. Naturally, she expected to steamroll her opponent in the decisive set. But for the third set in a row, Evert broke Navratilova in her first service game and jumped to the lead. Then Navratilova tied the score at three games all, but Evert broke and held for 5–3, and was serving for the match. Evert lost her serve, and Navratilova held to storm back to 5–5. Navratilova was on the verge of victory when she missed an easy shot. Evert recovered to hold serve, and, at last, after battling for close to three hours, she had match point on Navratilova's serve. When Evert hit a screaming backhand down the line to clinch the championship, Navratilova came around the net to hug her. "It's too bad someone had to win," said Navratilova

"IT'S TOO BAD SOMEONE HAD TO WIN": Navratilova with champion Evert at the 1985 French Open. Their battle for the title lasted close to three hours.

THE WILLIAMS SISTERS

Another female tennis rivalry features a pair of players who not only share a passion for winning—they share the same parents. The on-court tennis and sibling rivalry of the dominating duo of Serena and Venus Williams has riveted sports fans because the success of one sister has so often come at the expense of the other.

The Williams sisters have almost owned women's tennis since 1999, capturing 11 Grand Slam singles titles between them, through the 2005 Australian Open. Six times they have faced off against each other in the finals of a Grand Slam tournament. The younger Serena has won the last five times against Venus with a championship trophy on the line.

It's emotionally difficult to muster any acrimony against your opponent when that person across the net is your sister. Venus did win their initial sister vs. sister final at the 2001 U.S. Open, but her celebration was bittersweet. "I hate to see Serena lose—even against me," said Venus. "If she beats me, I'd maybe be happier. It's kind of strange . . . If I was playing a different opponent, I'd probably be a lot more joyful." The next year, the sisters became the first siblings in tennis history ever to rank one and two. At the 2002 French Open, Serena took another big step forward, winning her second Grand Slam singles title. However, she had to go through Venus to do it. After losing to her sister, Venus grabbed a camera and joined the hordes of photographers who were snapping pictures of Serena as she was posing with the championship trophy. The sisters laughed like the best friends that they are.

Serena captured the 2003 Australian Open for her fourth straight major title, completing what she called the "Serena Slam." Venus wasn't far behind, finishing as the runner-up to Serena for each of those championships.

"There's nothing like winning a Grand Slam," said Venus. "Serena and I, we both know that when we come out there, it's going to be two competitors competing against each other. That's just the way it is. When you walk out on the court, if you're not a competitor, you just got to go home. And we both understand that."

after her 65th match-up against Evert. "It was one of those matches that should go on forever."

Of course, nothing lasts forever. In 1992, three years after Evert's retirement, Navratilova broke her rival's all-time tennis singles record of 157 championships. They finished their careers tied with 18 Grand Slam singles titles each. They also finished their careers as they had started—as friends. After the two players retired, they each built houses in Aspen, Colorado. "We just can't seem to shake each other," Evert is fond of saying. "I think in the end," Evert continued, "we both realized that we pushed each other and made the other one a much better player."

When they started on the pro tour in the early 1970s, the women's tour offered a measly $300,000 in total purses because most tournaments drew such sparse crowds. By 1982, with their rivalry in full swing, the women's tour had grown to over $10 million in prize money and women players were consistently playing to packed houses. As Evert and Navratilova raised each other's game, they raised an entire sport.

—D.F.

LANCE ARMSTRONG *vs.* JAN ULLRICH

THE MOST GRUELING EVENT IN SPORTS IS THE EXHAUSTING 2,000-MILE TEST OF DESIRE KNOWN AS THE TOUR DE FRANCE. The most prestigious race in professional cycling, the Tour de France is a three-week ordeal of perspiration and agony. When it begins, the only obstacles standing between the riders and the finish line in Paris are two punishing mountain ranges: the Alps and Pyrenees. And then there's the temperature; racers have often wilted in the scorching heat in the sun-roasted south of France. Toss in occasional rain-slicked roads, crowds that mob the course just inches from riders, and descents that can send riders careening down mountain curves at 60 miles per hour. It's far from a gentle ride in the countryside. In the past decade, the century-old race has zoomed upward in world attention, and much of the credit for the sport's resurgence belongs to the cat-and-mouse game performed on two wheels by Lance Armstrong of the United States and Jan Ullrich of Germany.

Their battles began after Armstrong roared back from a bout with cancer to win his first Tour in 1999. Since then, the intense rivalry between Armstrong and Ullrich has transformed what the French call "Le Tour" into an annual battle of wills and skills. It has been a somewhat one-sided rivalry, however, with Armstrong winning an incredible six straight Tours since his first victory–while Ullrich has finished second five times (though he did win the 1997 edition of the race), including three times to Armstrong (2000, 2001, and 2003).

"My biggest rival is Jan Ullrich," said Armstrong before he won his unprecedented sixth Tour in a row, in 2004. "All the others are strong, but don't have Ullrich's potential."

Ullrich was the first of the pair to make a career breakthrough. A native of Rostock, Germany (in what was once East Germany), he is a product of that formerly Communist country's dominant sports machine. The powerful German was 22-years-old when he rode in his first Tour de France on the Deutche Telekom team, in 1996. His win the following year made him the first German ever to win the Tour.

And then there's Armstrong. After courageously and publicly battling back from testicular cancer just as he was

LESSONS IN
SPORTSMANSHIP

2001

- Stage 15, Ullrich crashes. Armstrong stops to wait.
- On the final day, Ullrich takes the winning Armstrong's hand as he crosses the finish line.
- Ullrich accepts champagne from the winner's team.

2003

- Stage 15, Armstrong crashes. Though he's dying to beat Armstrong, Ullrich stops to wait.

LIVING STRONG: Lance Armstrong on his way to a first Tour de France win, 1999. The inspirational victory came on the heels of Armstrong's cancer recovery.

attracting notice as a rider to watch, Armstrong became a national hero when he won the 1999 race. He won the first stage and avoided a major crash in stage two. He took the lead—and the fabled yellow jersey emblematic of the Tour leader—by calling on his greatest skill: climbing. Armstrong's ability to outrace and outclimb his rivals, ascending precariously steep roads with seemingly effortless strokes, separates him from the pack. Ullrich's speed and strength are also awesome, but pale in comparison to Armstrong's ability on hills. In 1999 the American stretched his lead during the three grueling mountain climbs Col de la Madeleine, Col du Glandon, and then L'Alpe d'Huez—an ascent so difficult it is called the "lair of eagles."

"Once I got back into racing, I could always draw strength from the fact that, no matter how hard things might look at a given moment, they could never be as hard as when I was back in Austin in a hospital bed with my hair falling out," he said, referring to the chemotheraphy that he underwent in his cancer battle. "I knew if I could beat cancer, I could get over any mountain."

Armstrong was not the first American to win the Tour de France. Greg LeMond, who won in 1986, then missed the 1987 and 1988 Tours due to serious injury, but came back to win in 1989 and 1990, accomplished that. But it was Armstrong who brought America's can-do attitude and a slew of new fans to a race that needed a dynamic champion after a doping scandal in 1998 had seriously damaged its international reputation.

Armstrong's victory in 1999 after his speedy recovery from cancer prompted some cynical cycling fans to question his training methods. Skeptics suspected that Armstrong's victory was made possible by performance-enhancing drugs. But he passed every random drug test and faced all the media scrutiny. Any doubt was laid to rest in 2000. The Tour field was stocked with the best in the world, and Armstrong rode them into the ground. He made an extraordinary charge early in the mountain stages

TURNING TIGHT: Lance Armstrong leads Jan Ullrich during Stage 13 of the 2001 Tour de France.

of the race that propelled him to his second yellow jersey. A week later he held an insurmountable lead, turning the final stage into a leisurely bike ride. Armstrong's second Tour victory, this time by a convincing six minutes and two seconds over Ullrich, quieted any lingering whispers that Armstrong's first victory had been a fluke.

"He was the strongest man, and he met our every attack. He earned this victory," said Ullrich. "Armstrong is a worthy champion."

Perhaps due to the changing of the guard, or perhaps because there was speculation that at 29 he was too old to win again, in 2001's Tour Armstrong uncharacteristically made an early surge to the overall lead, winning three of the first four stages. While Armstrong and Ullrich were riding together during a downhill portion of stage 13 from Foix to Saint-Lary-Soulan, Ullrich missed a left-hand turn and rode off the road, going over his handlebars before spilling into a grassy ravine in a nasty crash.

"I was going down at about 50 miles per hour and my brakes weren't working that well," said Ullrich, who quickly regained his feet.

Respecting the chivalry of the sport, Armstrong waited on the course until his chief rival remounted and returned to the race.

"I asked him if he was okay," said Armstrong. "It looked like a bad crash. I decided that the correct thing to do was to wait."

Then the Texan and the German champion rode off together, their mutual respect obvious to all. In the final stage Ullrich offered his hand to Armstrong and they crossed the finish line together. Though they ended this parade-like stage together, Armstrong was the Tour's overall winner by 6 minutes, 44 seconds over his main adversary. When it was over, Armstrong savored his success with a glass of champagne. Even Ullrich gulped down a glass offered by Armstrong's team manager.

STAT BOX

LANCE ARMSTRONG

BORN: SEPTEMBER 18, 1971, PLANO, TEXAS

TURNED PRO: 1992

TOUR DE FRANCE VICTORIES: 6

1999, 2000, 2001, 2002, 2003, 2004

JAN ULLRICH

BORN: DECEMBER 2, 1973, ROSTOCK, GERMANY

TURNED PRO: 1995

TOUR DE FRANCE VICTORIES: 1

1997

MOST TOUR DE FRANCE VICTORIES, ALL-TIME

LANCE ARMSTRONG	6	BERNARD HINAULT	5
MIGUEL INDURAIN	5	PHILIPPE THIJS	3
JACQUES ANQEUTIL	5	GREG LEMOND	3
EDDY MERCKX	5		

MARGINS OF VICTORY

1999: ARMSTRONG BEATS ULLRICH BY 6 MINUTES, 2 SECONDS

2001: ARMSTRONG BEATS ULLRICH BY 6 MINUTES, 44 SECONDS

2003: ARMSTRONG BEATS ULLRICH BY 61 SECONDS

SPORTSMEN AT THE FINISH: Lance Armstrong and Jan Ullrich hold hands while crossing the finish line of the Tour, 2001. Armstrong was again the winner.

"I tried everything that was possible," said Ullrich, seemingly resigned to his fate as second best. "I went to my limit, nothing more was possible. I have to wait for a black day for Armstrong, otherwise he is unbeatable."

The 2003 Tour saw their closest race ever, with Armstrong not assured of victory until the penultimate stage. Ullrich, returning from two knee operations and a ban for taking amphetamines, came into the Tour saying he did not expect to win. But as it became evident that Armstrong was suffering from severe dehydration and far from his best, the German pressured and attacked the Texan in the grueling mountain stages in the Alps.

But in the Pyrenees it was Armstrong who surged to a dramatic victory, quickly ascending over eight miles in one of the Tour's hardest climbs to reach the skiing village of Luz-Ardiden. Armstrong had recovered from a scary fall, caused by a spectator's outstretched handbag that caught his handlebars, and powered past Ullrich (who, in a gesture of sportsmanship mirroring Armstrong's two years before, waited for him to get back on his bike) to build a slim 67-second advantage. A time trial on the next-to-last day gave the rivalry its signature moment. In a time trial, riders race singly against the clock. Armstrong excels in these, but they are also Ullrich's strength. Here,

ON THE ROAD AGAIN: Armstrong and Ullrich race their closest Tour ever, 2003.

it seemed, was finally a chance for the German to defeat his rival. But just a short distance from the finish, Ullrich skidded on a rain-slicked patch and crashed. Though he quickly got up, the delay was enough to clinch yet another victory by Armstrong, though, at 61 seconds, it was his smallest margin of victory.

"I wanted to win this Tour," said a frustrated Ullrich. "I have never been so close to Armstrong."

Armstrong continues to attempt to add to his incredible records, while Ullrich seems to have settled for status as a mere demigod. Armstrong also continues to spread the message that he learned lying on that hospital bed, the message that he turns into inspirational success each summer on the hills and valleys of France. "My message now is: There is hope," said Armstrong. "Cancer isn't a death sentence. Survivors can go on, and they are better than they were before." Better, in Armstrong's case, than anyone has ever been before.

—D.F.

SPORTS KNOW-IT-ALL

MAILLOT
JAUNE

The yellow jersey, or the *maillot jaune*, is a Tour de France tradition that has been going on for 86 years. The first person to wear the yellow jersey was French rider Eugéne Christophe, in 1919. Then, as now, the yellow jersey is used to easily identify the overall race leader—the rider with the lowest accumulated time. The color yellow was chosen because it's the same color as the newspaper *L'Auto*, the race sponsor at the time.

Actually, the yellow jersey is only one of four jerseys riders compete to wear throughout the Tour. The others are: the maillot blanc or the white jersey, awarded to the rider under 25 years old with the lowest accumulated time; the maillot vert or the green jersey, awarded to the best sprinter; and the maillot á pois or the polka-dot jersey, worn by the best climber.

The Tour de France's all-time leaders in days spent in the yellow jersey:
96 – Eddy Merckx
78 – Bernard Hinault
66 – Lance Armstrong
60 – Miguel Indurain
51 – Jacques Anquetil

CUBS *vs.* CARDINALS

THE RIVALRY BETWEEN THE CHICAGO CUBS AND ST. LOUIS CARDINALS, STRETCHING BACK TO THE 19TH CENTURY, HAS BEEN marked mostly by midwestern gentility, although recent events have added a hint of derision. The Cardinals are by far the more successful team of the two; in fact, St. Louis holds the N.L. record with nine World Series wins, second overall only to the Yankees. The Cubs, meanwhile, are forever cursed, the lovable losers, seemingly destined to bridesmaid status. They haven't even been to the World Series since 1945 and haven't won since 1908!

For all of its one-sidedness, the geographical connection and longtime N.L. pairing of the two franchises has created a sense of shared community among the team's fans. While Chicago actually shares its hometown with another team, the White Sox, they're in the American League and have only recently begun to play the Cubs during the regular season (they did face off in the only all-Chicago World Series in 1906, won by the then–White Stockings). So it is their neighbors to the south who bear the brunt of Cubs fans' long-lasting, not enmity exactly . . . let's just say, healthy choruses of boos.

The Cubs were actually the first of the pair to have significant success. The Cubbies are the oldest franchise in the N.L., having represented Chicago (though under different nicknames) since 1871. They won the N.L. pennant seven times from 1907 through 1938. However, though they won it all in the 1907 and 1908 Series, they lost every other time they reached the Fall Classic. They made it again in 1945 and ain't been there since.

The Cardinals began life as the St. Louis Brown Stockings of the American Association in 1881 and didn't sniff a Series until the 1920s. They then began a pattern of fairly consistent success, winning Series titles through 1989 in every decade except the 1950s and 1970s. The Cardinals also boasted a parade of Hall of Famers such as Rogers Hornsby, Stan Musial, and Bob Gibson.

In terms of head-to-head rivalry, there are few notable match-ups until after World War II. With geography egging them on, their meetings began to generate more fan interest than games against other N.L. teams, and the players made a point of playing a little harder against each other. In 1952 Musial was competing for a batting title against Cubbie Frank Baumholtz. In a move that today would be met with anger and finger-pointing, outfielder Musial good-naturedly took the mound to pitch to Baumholtz one time, the Cubs batter reached on an error, and Musial went on to win the batting title. Six years later, Musial also collected his 3,000th career hit in a game against the Cubs.

The two teams also engaged in perhaps the most abysmal and one-sided trade in baseball history. Unheralded journeyman pitcher Ernie Broglio was sent to the Cubs by the Cardinals in exchange for a young outfielder named Lou Brock. All Brock did was lead the Cards to three World Series appearances, set a new all-time record

> THE TWO TEAMS ENGAGED IN PERHAPS THE MOST ABYSMAL AND ONE-SIDED TRADE IN BASEBALL HISTORY.

HALL OF FAME HITTER: Stan Musial of the St. Louis Cardinals watches the flight of his ball, 1957.

STAT BOX

FIRST GAME

APRIL 12, 1892

LIFETIME HEAD-TO-HEAD RECORD

CUBS 1,044–CARDINALS 1,014

WORLD SERIES TITLES

CUBS: 2

1907, 1908

CARDINALS: 9

1926, 1931, 1934, 1942,

1944, 1946, 1964, 1967,

1982

GREATEST PLAYERS

CUBS

GROVER CLEVELAND ALEXANDER

ERNIE BANKS

MORDECAI BROWN

RYNE SANDBERG

HACK WILSON

CARDINALS

LOU BROCK

BOB GIBSON

ROGERS HORNSBY

STAN MUSIAL

OZZIE SMITH

THE NAME GAME

CUBS

1871–1898: THE CHICAGO COLTS

1898–1902: THE ORPHANS

1902-PRESENT: THE CUBS

CARDINALS

1881–1899: THE ST. LOUIS BROWNS

1899–1900: THE PERFECTOS

1900-PRESENT: THE CARDINALS

for stolen bases with 938, post a career batting average of .293, and earn a spot in the Hall of Fame. Broglio . . . didn't. Cubs fans point to the trade as a symbol of how the breaks just never seem to go their way.

They point to 1969 as another example, when Chicago led the new N.L. East by eight games in late August, only to collapse and watch the New York "Miracle" Mets get hot and win the title. Once again, Cubs fans went home disappointed.

Following that season, the two teams made another kind of trade, as longtime Cardinals broadcaster Harry Caray headed north to take over as the voice of the Cubs. Perhaps no other personality in team history—not Hall of Famers Ernie Banks or Ryne Sandberg—was more loved than Caray, a voluble, cartoonish announcer. His in-game renditions of "Take Me Out to the Ballgame" have become a Wrigley Field staple, and his cry of "Cubs win! Cubs win!" was one of baseball's most familiar. Caray was the voice and face of the team until his death in 1998. Staying behind in St. Louis was Caray's old partner, Jack Buck, who became in his own way as much a part of the Cardinals as Caray was part of the Cubs. More laid-back than the sometimes-outlandish Caray (who would doff his shirt and sit in the bleachers to call a game), Buck became a legend in St. Louis and a broadcaster of national acclaim.

Both teams endured a dry spell in the 1970s, but in 1984, the Cubs put together a team that is still talked about around Chicago. And one of the key moments that season came in a game at Wrigley against the Cardinals.

It was on July 11 and the Cubs were fighting for first place. The Cardinals' great outfielder Willie McGee put on a real batting show, hitting for the cycle and helping the Cards score 11 runs. However, the Cubs' Ryne "Ryno" Sandberg hit a homer in the bottom of the ninth to tie the game. He slugged another in the 11th for a 12–11 Cubs win. The Cubs held on to win the division that season, but lost three straight games in the NLCS after winning the first two. As usual, there went the Cubs' fans, disappointed.

SAFE!: Lou Brock of the St. Louis Cardinals steals second base, 1965.

In 1989 the Cubs again used a victory against the Cardinals to spur them to a division crown, putting together a three-game sweep in September that cinched the deal. Of course, they collapsed in the playoffs.

The summer of 1998 marked the next key milestones in the rivalry, as the Cardinals' Mark McGwire and the Cubs' Sammy Sosa engaged in a home-run-race duel for the ages (see box page 143). Big Mac and Sosa hugged after McGwire finally broke the single-season record with his 62nd homer. Those were the last hugs we're likely to see in this rivalry, though, because in 2003, along came Dusty Baker.

A bit of background: As manager of the Giants in 2002, Baker had tussled verbally (and nearly physically) with Cardinals' manager Tony LaRussa. Skip to 2003 and

IN 1984, THE CUBS PUT TOGETHER A TEAM THAT IS STILL TALKED ABOUT AROUND CHICAGO.

SMILING RIVALS: Rivals in the home run race and playing for archrival clubs, Sammy Sosa and Mark McGwire were all smiles at one of the press conferences they held during that magical 1998 season.

Baker is in the Cubs' dugout, it's late in the season, and the Cardinals are in town for a key five-game series. Tossing a century of good-hearted rivalry out the window, the two teams went at each other tooth-and-nail. There were several near-beanings, a near-fight between the managers, and some very nasty talk by players and fans alike.

The Cardinals watched, then, with extra glee as the Cubs (again!) self-destructed in the playoffs. Fan interference on a key foul ball led to a rally by the Florida Marlins. The Cubs, once five outs from their first Series appearance since 1945, were again disappointed.

The rancor continued in 2004, with Cubs pitcher Carlos Zambrano zinging a few pitches near the head of Cardinals slugger Jim Edmonds in a July series. The next game featured a real reversal of fortune for the Cubs, with eerie shades of Sandberg. At home against

the Cubbies, the Cardinals trailed 8–2 after only three innings. But in a reverse of the 1984 events, this time it was a Cardinal slugger who saved the day. The remarkable Albert Pujols smacked three homers, drove in six runs, and led the Cards to a thrilling, come-from-behind 11–8 victory. Observers point to that game as the springboard on their drive to the division crown.

Thanks in part to the fact that both clubs are among baseball's best, and with a soupçon of dust-ups from Dusty, the rivalry is fiercer now than it has ever been. "Players get into it because the fans are into it, too," said Joe Buck, former Cardinals announcer turned national FOX play-by-play man (and son of Jack Buck). "You can't help but feel the energy when you walk into the packed stadium."

—J.B.

MAC & SAMMY

Would the wonderful summer of 1998 have been any less wonderful if Mark McGwire had played for, say, the Brewers and Sammy Sosa for the Padres? Yes, it probably would have dulled somewhat. That these two sluggers literally revitalized baseball during their titanic home-run summer of '98 was a fact no doubt enhanced by the fact that they played for two old rivals. How perfect was it that when Big Mac finally slugged No. 62 to break Roger Maris's single-season record, Sammy Sosa was in right field and could sprint in to congratulate his rival in roundtrippers?

The home run race of 1998 seemed to come almost out of nowhere. Many expected McGwire to continue to challenge Maris's mark; Big Mac whacked 58 homers in 1997. But Sosa's participation was electric; heading into June that year, McGwire had 27 homers and Sosa only 14. By the end of the month, Sosa had set a single-month record with 20, nearly caught McGwire, and the chase was on.

Throughout July and August, the two players were the single focus of the sports world, and the wider news world as well. Their every swing was followed by millions. Baseball was still reeling in some ways from the disastrous 1994 season in which labor troubles had forced the cancellation of the World Series for only the first time since 1904. So the two players, so sunny and strong and sportsmanlike, were big-biceped rays of hope for the game and its fans.

Big Mac made it to 62 first, on September 7, setting off a huge celebration that included Sosa's hug. By September 13, Sosa, too, had topped Maris. But McGwire finished the strongest, with two homers in the season's final game to reach his then-record of 70. Sosa, however, led the Cubs to the playoffs and was the N.L. MVP.

The legacy of that summer, however, has been sullied by the ongoing debate about steroids. While McGwire admitted to using a then-legal supplement known as "andro," his abysmal 2005 appearance at Congressional hearings can't fail to cast a pall on his records. There is no way to know for certain whether McGwire used steroids to enhance his skills, but there is also no way to know for certain that he did not. For his part, Sosa was caught using a corked bat in 2003 and after declaring that he would take a steroid test anytime, anywhere, refused to do just that.

RANGERS *vs.* ISLANDERS

NEW YORK CITY HAS A LOT GOING FOR IT—GREAT RESTAURANTS, BROADWAY SHOWS, A RICH MAYOR . . . PLUS, IT'S THE the only city in the United States that boasts two National Hockey League teams. Well, sort of. One half of the rivalry has been skating in the Big Apple since 1926; the other half is the newcomer and plays its games on the landmass from which it takes its name: The rivalry between the old-guard, midtown New York Rangers and the expansion-era, bridge-and-tunnel New York Islanders is as intense as they come. And if you disagree, they'll see you by the corner boards, gloves off.

The Rangers had had the New York hockey scene pretty much to themselves for 50 years before the NHL added an expansion team on Long Island for the 1972–73 season. But for much of that time, the Rangers lived in the league basement. In fact, during the 25 years of the Original Six era (1942–1967), New York missed the playoffs 18 times. But under the leadership of coach Emile Francis, the Rangers were on the rise as the Islanders came into being. With Ed Giacomin in goal, Brad Park on defense, and the Goal-A-Game Line of Rod Gilbert, Jean Ratelle, and Vic Hadfield leading the offense, the team became a powerhouse in the early 1970s. During the spring of '72, the Rangers reached the Finals for just the second time since winning the Stanley Cup in 1940. However, Lord Stanley's trophy eluded them thanks to Bobby Orr, Phil Esposito, and the Boston Bruins.

The 1972 Stanley Cup series wrapped up on May 11. Less than a month later, on June 6, 1972, the NHL officially welcomed the Islanders into the fold. Cost of the franchise was $6 million, but $4 million would have to be paid to the Rangers as a territorial fee, for "encroaching" on the older team's historic base. A few months later, the Rangers and Islanders inaugurated the Islanders' new home, the Nassau County Coliseum, in an exhibition game the Rangers won 6–4. During the regular season, the Rangers won all six meetings between the two clubs and outscored the Islanders 25–5. Just another few bricks in the wall of futility the Islanders built in 1972–1973, when they set all-time NHL lows with a record of 12–60–6 and just 30 points. Meanwhile, the Rangers were 47–23–8 for 102 points.

"Hapless was the word," Islanders' general manager Bill Torrey told author Stan Fischler. "The Rangers play the hapless Islanders tonight. Cripes, I though hapless was the only word in the English language."

But the upside of a hapless season was the opportunity to select Denis Potvin with the first choice in the 1973 Entry Draft. Potvin became the foundation around which Torrey and coach Al Arbour built the Islanders, and the NHL Draft was where the team would continue to find its talent.

After a second season that had been little better than their first, the Islanders suddenly improved to an 88-point performance in year three. They not only qualified for the playoffs, but they were paired up with their New York rivals in the best-of-three opening round. Still, few Rangers fans, and not many players, took the Islanders seriously.

"Make no mistake," remembered Potvin, "a lot of those Rangers' players gave us the business about how good they supposedly were and how easy it was to beat us." But Potvin believed the high-priced Rangers played for the money and nothing else. "The Rangers never showed me that extra tenaciousness that the Canadiens or the Bruins have always had," he wrote in his 1977 autobiography *Power on Ice*. "They didn't have the mean streak that would make them want to beat an enemy badly."

STICK-TO-STICK: New York Islanders' Denis Potvin (left) battles with New York Rangers' Ulf Nilsson during the 1981 NHL playoffs.

OVERTIME SHOT: J. P. Parise of the Islanders scores a goal in overtime to defeat the Rangers in the first round of the 1975 Stanley Cup playoffs.

The Islanders' strategy for the 1975 series was to outhustle and outhit the Rangers. The result was a 3–2 Islanders victory at Madison Square Garden in Game One. The Rangers bounced back for an impressive 8–3 win at Nassau Coliseum in Game Two, and when they rallied from a 3–0 deficit at home in Game Three it appeared they really might have the right stuff. However, just 11 seconds into overtime, J. P. Parise put the puck past Eddie Giacomin, and the Islanders had a series victory.

After only three years as the "up-and-coming" young team in this Big Apple battle, the Islanders had come on up.

WITH POTVIN, TROTTIER, AND BOSSY leading the way, the Islanders challenged the Canadiens, Bruins, Sabres, and Flyers for the top spot in hockey over the next four years while the Rangers desperately tried to retool. But good as they were in the regular season, the Islanders were gaining the reputation as a team that couldn't go all the way. The cross-island rival Rangers certainly helped to drive home that point in 1979.

In the 1979 playoffs, the Rangers showed the kids that they still had a few tricks up their sweaters and kept the Islanders from advancing. The Islanders had finished in first place overall in 1978–79 with a record of 51–15–14 and 116 points. They then swept Chicago in the quarterfinals to set up a semifinal matchup with the Rangers, who had finished 25 points behind them in the Patrick Division standings. It didn't look so much like a playoff series as a potential coronation of a new big dog on Broadway. "We're up against the best team in the league," said Rangers coach Fred Shero before Game One, "but we'll show up and try and make a series of it."

Tickets to the so-called Expressway Series were selling for as much as $150 per game and those who paid it watched Rangers goalie John Davidson put on the performance of a lifetime.

"You can make every kind of excuse," said Bob Nystrom, "but when a goalie stones you the way Davidson did, there isn't much else to say." The Rangers took the series in six games. It is of such upsets and surprises

STAT BOX

FIRST GAME

OCTOBER 21, 1972 • RANGERS 2–ISLANDERS 1

LIFETIME HEAD-TO-HEAD RECORD

RANGERS 88–ISLANDERS 84 (19 TIES)

STANLEY CUP CHAMPIONSHIPS

RANGERS: 4

1928, 1933, 1940, 1994

ISLANDERS: 4

1980, 1981, 1982, 1983

TOP CAREER GOAL SCORERS

RANGERS

ROD GILBERT (406)

JEAN RATELLE (336)

ADAM GRAVES (280)

ANDY BATHGATE (272)

VIC HADFIELD (262)

ISLANDERS

MIKE BOSSY (573)

BRYAN TROTTIER (500)

DENIS POTVIN (310)

CLARK GILLES (304)

PAT LAFONTAINE AND

BRENT SUTTER (287)

RETIRED NUMBERS

RANGERS

EDDIE GIACOMIN (#1),

ROD GILBERT (#7)

ISLANDERS

DENIS POTVIN (#5), CLARK GILLES

(#9), BRYAN TROTTIER (#19), MIKE

BOSSY (#22), BOB NYSTROM

(#23), BILLY SMITH (#31)

HIGHLIGHT REEL

★ ★ ★ ★ ★

1942–1962: The Era of the Original Six

During much of this time period, the Montreal Canadiens, Toronto Maple Leafs, Detroit Red Wings, New York Rangers, Boston Bruins, and Chicago Black Hawks played against each other 14 times per year, breeding a familiarity—and contempt—that is impossible to imagine today.

1967: Expansion begins

Expansion began in 1967 and has seen the NHL grow from 6 to 30 teams, leading to other new rivalries. During the 1980s, the Battle of Quebec between the Canadiens and Nordiques was every bit as exciting as the wars that raged between Montreal and Toronto in the 1960s. At the same time the Habs and Nordiques were fighting for the honor of *la belle province*, the Calgary Flames and Edmonton Oilers were waging the Battle of Alberta in the Canadian west.

1980s: Era of Fire and Oil

The Flames and (especially) the Oilers dominated the Stanley Cup in the 1980s. In fact, one of those two teams played in the Finals for eight straight seasons from 1983 until 1990, with the Oilers winning the Cup in 1984, 1985, 1987, 1988, and 1990, and the Flames winning in 1989. It was a pretty good bet that whichever one of those two teams survived what seemed like their annual playoff battle in the old Smythe Division was going to be sipping champagne come season's end.

DÉJÀ VU: The Islanders celebrate Ken Morrow's overtime goal against the Rangers in the semifinals, 1984.

that great rivalries are made.

Both New York teams slipped a bit in the standings in 1979–80, but Bill Torrey's late-season acquisition of Butch Goring from Los Angeles—plus Ken Morrow joining the team fresh off the 1980 United States Olympic Miracle on Ice victory—gave the Islanders a lift heading into the playoffs. "With Butchie at center," Potvin later recalled, "there was a sense of hope we didn't have before." The revitalized Islanders went all the way to the Finals, beating Philadelphia on Bob Nystrom's overtime goal in Game Six to win the Stanley Cup. Just like that, the disappointment the Rangers caused a year earlier evaporated, and the Stanley Cup, like so many other New Yorkers, went out to Long Island to spend the summer.

It had taken the Islanders just eight years to win hockey's ultimate prize—something the Rangers had been unable to do in 40. And as the Islanders won championship after championship over the next three years (including—ouch—beating the Rangers in the playoffs en route to the Finals every year), a new dimension was added to the rivalry. Islanders fans would chant "19–40!" every time the Rangers came to visit, a mocking reference

to the fact that the Broadway Blueshirts had not won the Stanley Cup since then. Rangers' fans replied by tormenting their most hated opponent with the chant of "Potvin Sucks!" (a cry that can still be heard on occasion in the highest seats at Madison Square Garden).

A Ken Morrow overtime goal in 1984 gave the Islanders a fourth straight playoff victory over their cross-town rivals, but there would be little glory on Long Island after that. The Rangers have won the teams' only two playoff meetings since then, including a lopsided 4–0 sweep (the Rangers outscored the Islanders 22–3) that began their run to the 1994 Stanley Cup. Watching Mark Messier, Mike Richter, Brian Leetch, and company end their team's 54-year Stanley Cup drought was the dream of a lifetime for many Rangers fans. But, as authors John Kreiser and Lou Friedman wrote in their 1996 book *The New York Rangers: Broadway's Longest Running Hit*, "beating the Islanders to start the trip to the championship made it just a little more special for most Ranger fans."

—ERIC ZWEIG

Eric Zweig is the managing editor of *Total Hockey*, the official NHL Encyclopedia.

JACK NICKLAUS *vs.* ARNOLD PALMER

RIVALS IN GOLF HAVE IT A LITTLE DIFFERENT THAN THOSE IN OTHER INDIVIDUAL SPORTS. BJORN BORG COULD SMASH a forehand at John McEnroe. Muhammad Ali had a jab to lay on Joe Frazier. Even in a team sport, Bill Russell had to guard Wilt Chamberlain. But in golf, you compete against the course and against par, and can only hope that your rival doesn't do as well. It's a mind game, too, of course, and you want to be the guy who is so feared by the rival that he makes a mistake, that he thinks too much and lets emotion affect his swing or his game.

For most of the 1960s, the greatest rivals in golf were also two of the greatest players the sport has ever known.

ARNOLD PALMER was the antithesis of the elite country club golfer. He was Everyman with a sand wedge, Joe Muni playing with the big boys. His easy smile, his crooked swing, his pained grimaces, all made golf fans love him, win or lose—though he did more than his share of winning. After a great college golf career at Wake Forest and a stint in the Coast Guard, he came back to the game he had grown up with (he lived on the 6th hole of Latrobe (Pennsylvania) Country Club, where his dad was the superintendent). After winning the 1954 U.S. Amateur title, he turned pro and started winning quickly.

In 1958 he won the first of his major tournament titles, the fabled Masters Invitational at Augusta, Georgia. He won it again in 1960, finishing with birdies on the final two holes to grab a stunning one-shot victory. The same year, at the U.S. Open at Cherry Hills in Denver, he

> ## "I DIDN'T WIN . . . NOBODY EVER REMEMBERS WHO FINISHED SECOND AT ANYTHING"
> ## —JACK NICKLAUS, 1960

trailed by a surely insurmountable seven strokes entering the final round. To the delight of the growing crowd of fans that were following him, he drove the first green and made eagle, starting one of the great final rounds in golf history. Palmer put up a stunning 65 and overcame Mike Souchak to win the Open. (Two shots behind that day was Nicklaus, Palmer's future nemesis.) Arnie's come-from-behind exploits there and at other tournaments added another reason for hero-starved golf fans to jump on the Palmer bandwagon. There were so many that soon they became—and remain—"Arnie's Army."

Palmer won British Open titles in 1961 and 1962 as well, along with 29 PGA tournaments between 1960 and 1963. By the time he captured his fourth Masters (and final major title) in 1964, he had won more money playing golf than any player in history.

Meanwhile, another golfer was creeping up the ladder, preparing his own assault on the Army's hero. Nicklaus had started early, breaking 70 by age 13 and becoming the youngest winner of the U.S. Amateur in half a century, winning at the age of 19 in 1959. After finishing two strokes behind Palmer at the U.S. Open the next year, the year of Palmer's famous charge, Nicklaus was not happy. "I didn't win," he said. "Nobody ever remembers who finished second at anything." He turned pro in 1961.

Nicklaus' talent was so obvious that before the 1962 U.S. Open at Oakmont in Pennsylvania, Palmer was

FORMIDABLE NEWCOMER: Jack Nicklaus, right, and Arnold Palmer shake hands at the U.S. Open, 1962. Nicklaus exploded onto the scene when he won this event, his first career Major.

PASSING THE COAT: Palmer helps Nicklaus don his Masters blazer, 1963, in a tradition whereby the previous year's winner helps the new one put on the famous green jacket.

quoted as referring to his future rival by heft, if not by name. "Everybody says there's only one favorite, and that's me," he said. "But you'd better watch the fat boy."

Palmer, the favorite, was right where he was supposed to be heading into the final turn on Sunday. He was up by five strokes on the "fat boy," but that was not enough. With a stunning final-nine charge, Nicklaus made up all five strokes and forced a one-round playoff for the Open title. In the 18-hole playoff the next day, the kid knocked off the champ, ten years his senior, winning by three strokes. Nicklaus had arrived and a rivalry began.

"Now that the big guy's out of the cage, everybody better run for cover," Palmer said at the time.

After that, the rivalry grew larger and more important, with each big tournament seen as a battle between "Fat

Jack" and "Arnie and his Army," with a Gary Player or Lee Trevino thrown into the mix occasionally.

"At times we became so hyper about beating each other that we let someone else go right by us and win," Palmer said later. "But our competition was good and fun for the game."

The sort of invective seen in other sports rivalries was mostly absent in this golfing match-up—no pre-match poetry, no clubhouse brawls, no finger-pointing. This was a more genteel rivalry, though within the confines of the Rules of Golf, no less intense than other such clashes.

That didn't stop the press from doing its part to fan the flames. Nicklaus was not the sleek, golden-maned athlete of his more mature years. This young golfer was, well, pudgy, his fuzzy crewcut topping off a face that

STAT BOX

ARNOLD PALMER

BORN: SEPTEMBER 10, 1929, LATROBE, PENNSYLVANIA

TURNED PRO: 1954

PGA TOUR WINS: 62

MAJOR CHAMPIONSHIPS: 7

MASTERS: 1958, 1960, 1962, 1964

U.S. OPEN: 1960

BRITISH OPEN: 1961, 1962

CAREER HOLES-IN-ONE IN TOURNAMENT PLAY: 16

BEST 4–ROUND TOTAL AT THE MASTERS: 276 IN 1964

BEST 4–ROUND TOTAL AT U.S. OPEN: 278 IN 1966

JACK NICKLAUS

BORN: JANUARY 21, 1940, COLUMBUS, OHIO

TURNED PRO: 1961

PGA TOUR WINS: 73

MAJOR CHAMPIONSHIPS: 18

MASTERS: 1963, 1965, 1966, 1972, 1975, 1986

U.S. OPEN: 1962, 1967, 1972, 1980

BRITISH OPEN: 1966, 1970, 1978

PGA CHAMPIONSHIP: 1963, 1971, 1973, 1975, 1980

CAREER HOLES-IN-ONE IN TOURNAMENT PLAY: 19

BEST 4–ROUND TOTAL AT THE MASTERS: 271 IN 1965

BEST 4–ROUND TOTAL AT U.S. OPEN: 272 IN 1980*

(*TIED WITH THREE OTHERS FOR LOWEST EVER)

ANOTHER KIND
OF COMPETITION

Nicklaus outstripped Palmer in majors, total victories, and money won. He's also slightly ahead of his old rival in another game: golf course construction. Palmer created the Palmer Golf Course Design Company with Ed Seay in 1971, and they have since had a hand in more than 250 courses. Nicklaus started with a coproduction with Pete Dye at Harbour Town in South Carolina, in 1969. Since then, while still extensive, Palmer's coursework has just been a small, modest part of a wider commercial empire that has made him one of the world's wealthiest sportsmen.

Nicklaus's design and construction business, meanwhile, has boomed, and his courses can now be found in 28 countries. More than 230 courses have been built or partially designed with the famous Nicklaus name, and 50-plus more have come out of his company, Nicklaus Design. The Golden Bear himself often plays the first official round on his brand-new courses.

However, while Nicklaus has Palmer beat in courses designed, Palmer owns the Golden Bear in another competition: In 2004, Palmer was 19th on Forbes' annual list of highest-paid athletes. At the age of 75, he made more than $20 million through his many endorsements. Not bad for an old "Army" man.

had not known Atkins. "Fat Jack," they all called him (a *Sports Illustrated* cover branded him, un-politically-correctly, as "A Whale of a Golfer"), and his business-like, intense demeanor contrasted somewhat sharply with the glad-handing "man of the people" that Palmer embodied. Their games looked different, too. Palmer was the scrambler, the shotmaker who had to use every club in his bag, and sometimes in odd and different ways, to put up his scores. Nicklaus was perhaps golf's first boomer, a powerful young player who drove it long, chipped it close, and with that famous severe and statue-like deliberation, rolled home putt after putt. His sole expression until victory seemed to be a grimace, while Palmer's face and body language told how he was feeling after every shot, good or bad.

That win at the Open in 1962 began a remarkable decade for the young man from Ohio. Another key moment came in 1963, when he won his first Masters. In a symbol not lost on either golfer or observers of the time, the defending champ was Palmer. Masters tradition dictates that the previous champ help the new champ with the game's most famous trophy, the green jacket of a Masters champ.

Though he was the reigning king of the game, Palmer was astute enough at that moment to see the future. He wrote in his 1999 book, *A Golfer's Life*, "I was suddenly staring at the future and my greatest rival in the game. It was an emotional moment, bittersweet for me. Jack Nicklaus had come of age, and professional golf would never be the same."

After Arnold helped Jack with his new wardrobe, Palmer won only one more major; Nicklaus added 16, including five more Masters, the most ever. The torch had not just been passed, it had disappeared into the distance.

(Ironically, as Nicklaus pointed out in a 2004 interview, Augusta was almost never the site of one of their big battles. "Arnold and I have been linked at the hip with Augusta, and I'm sure always will be. What's amazing, though, is that of the combination of ten Masters [titles] between us, we never really went down to the wire to decide the tournament." Arnie and Jack were 1–2 in 1964, but Palmer led by six strokes. Jack returned the favor in 1965, but romped by nine shots.)

The rivalry continued, but more as a part of history than a part of actual competition. By the late 1960s,

FRIENDLY RIVALS: Palmer and Nicklaus share a joke during the Masters as caddies look on, 1987.

Nicklaus had bypassed Palmer as golf's finest all-around player and was steaming ahead in his drive to become the best ever. That didn't stop either golfer from expecting fireworks when they met in a tournament.

On his Web site, Nicklaus reflects on the rivalry, looking back on its long and varied history. "Our rivalry has always been wonderfully competitive, but never bitter," he writes. "It was and still is a friendly rivalry. I consider Arnold one of my closest friends in the game. That doesn't mean that every time we went out there, we didn't want to beat each other's brains in. We're both competitors— always have been and always will be."

"We enjoyed each other's company and enjoyed playing against each other," Palmer recalled in 2004. "We had a lot of fun doing it and we still compete on the links. We're driven hard . . . that's part of us."

Their rivalry continues today even though their games are not the powerhouses they once were. Each has played, often against the other, most winters in the past two decades in a Skins Game. Arnie hasn't won much in these "silly season" events, but Jack has often added several thousand dollars to his bulging wallet. They still go at it with all they've got left.

"Even 40 years after we started, we're still trying to drum each other," Nicklaus said before the 2005 event. "Every time we play now, it's fun and special because you never know how much golf we'll play together."

—J.B.

BJORN BORG VS. JOHN McENROE

THE ATMOSPHERE WAS A LITTLE LIKE ALI VS. FRAZIER AT THE GARDEN. OR PERHAPS PALMER VS. NICKLAUS AT OAKMONT. Two premier players hooked up in the final match of the Wimbledon men's singles championships in 1980, and about 15,000 people crammed into the quaint Centre Court at the All-England Club to witness an electrifying tennis rivalry that with forward spin would soon unfold into one of the most heralded in all of sports.

In this corner, exuding confidence as the reigning Wimbledon champion, 24-year-old Bjorn Borg of Sweden, who dominated men's tennis in the late 1970s with the fluid movement and pinpoint topspin baseline strokes that were his trademark. In the other corner, from Douglaston, Queens, an affluent suburb of New York, John McEnroe, 21, whose high-kicking, left-handed serve and ability to win points by fearlessly charging the net would soon carry him to the top of the rankings in the early 1980s.

The Wimbledon final of 1980 was to be Borg's last hurrah. The fourth set concluded with a dramatic 34-point tiebreaker that went to McEnroe after he had survived seven match points. The scrappy New Yorker prevailed, 18–16, in a tiebreaker that lasted 22 minutes (five more than the entire first set) to deadlock the thrilling match. Then Borg, displaying the composure and resolve that were the keys to his success, reclaimed lost momentum, telling himself: "Don't give up; don't get tight."

In the deciding set it was Borg's serve that made the difference. Although he lost the first two points in the first game of the fifth set, he did not lose another point on serve until the tenth game, an incredible string of 19 points in a row. Borg's consistency and determination finally wore down his opponent, though McEnroe yielded reluctantly. Like well-conditioned fighters, they had been trading shots for three hours and 53 minutes.

The end came in the 54th minute. From 15-all, Borg hit three straight passing shots to win the fifth set and his fifth consecutive All-England title.

"For sure, it is the best match I have ever played at Wimbledon," said Borg after winning his record 35th singles match in a row.

HIGHLIGHT REEL
★★★★★

Wimbledon, 1980
Borg defeated McEnroe in a year that many thought that the left-handed American might finally knock off the "unbeatable" Swede.

U.S. Open, 1980
McEnroe got some revenge by defeating Borg to win his second straight U.S. Open title.

Wimbledon, 1981
In a match featuring some of the greatest back-and-forth action in the tournament's long history, McEnroe finally broke Borg's five-championship string.

SWEDISH PHENOM: Bjorn Borg drops to his knees after beating John McEnroe to win his fifth successive men's singles title at Wimbledon, 1980.

CALL HIM McENRONEY: A patriotic John McEnroe serves during his Wimbledon match against Bjorn Borg, July 4, 1981.

McEnroe got his wish to avenge his Wimbledon defeat by meeting the Swede in September in the final of the U.S. Open tournament, played in Flushing Meadows, New York, near McEnroe's hometown. The local favorite got off quickly and won the first two sets, but Borg showed his championship mettle by coming back to capture the next two sets. Since 1976, when Borg had been down two-sets-to-love and then come back to force a deciding fifth set, he had triumphed over McEnroe in 13 straight matches, but this match would end the streak. McEnroe went the distance and won the four-hour, 13-minute endurance test in five sets.

The two players were a spectacular clash of contrasting styles. The Swedish sensation was reserved, gentlemanly, and steely cool. His lack of any outward reaction to events both good and bad prompted commentators to wonder if he had any emotions at all. McEnroe, who had a potent serve and was a crafty shot maker, was well known for his terrific talent and his terrible temper on the tennis court. He demanded perfection of himself and those around him, and when he didn't get it, he screamed at officials and threw temper tantrums after unforced errors.

Similarly, both players combined powerful groundstrokes with a nifty touch, deftly dissecting their opponents—and each other—with a wooden racquet. Their heated competition did not last as long as the 15-year rivalry between Chris Evert and Martina Navratilova (see page 124)—between 1978 and '81, McEnroe and Borg played just 14 matches, and each player won seven. But the atmosphere surrounding their four epic battles in the finals of Wimbledon and the U.S. Open in 1980 and '81 resembled heavyweight boxing championship bouts—and ultimately it would be McEnroe delivering the knockout punches.

McEnroe and Borg were once again the main attraction on the hallowed lawn of the British championships of 1981. The date of the Wimbledon final happened to fall on July 4—Independence Day back in the colonies—so McEnroe appeared on court dressed in blue and white with a red headband.

"Stick a feather in his cap and call him McEnroney," quipped the sportscaster Bud Collins.

McEnroe had set the All-England Club abuzz by famously referring to Wimbledon as "the pits of the world." The explosive New Yorker's mouth caused even

STAT BOX

FIRST MEETING

NOVEMBER 12, 1978 • McENROE WON 6–3, 6–4

LIFETIME HEAD-TO-HEAD RECORD

BORG 7–McENROE 7

JOHN McENROE

BORN: FEBRUARY 18, 1959, WEISBADEN, WEST GERMANY

ALL-TIME SINGLES TOURNAMENT VICTORIES: 77

GRAND SLAM CHAMPIONSHIPS: 7

WIMBLEDON: 1981, 1983, 1984

U.S. OPEN: 1979, 1980, 1981, 1984

OTHER ACHIEVEMENTS:

WIMBLEDON DOUBLES TITLES: 5

U.S. OPEN DOUBLES TITLES: 4

INDUCTED INTO HALL OF FAME IN 1999

BJORN BORG

BORN: JUNE 6, 1956, SÖDERTÄLJE, SWEDEN

ALL-TIME SINGLES TOURNAMENT VICTORIES: 62

GRAND SLAM CHAMPIONSHIPS: 11

FRENCH OPEN: 1974, 1975, 1978, 1979, 1980, 1981

WIMBLEDON: 1976, 1977, 1978, 1979, 1980

OTHER ACHIEVEMENTS:

AT 17, YOUNGEST WINNER OF THE ITALIAN CHAMPIONSHIP

INDUCTED INTO HALL OF FAME IN 1987

LOVE TRIANGLE

CONNORS ON McENROE:

"My two-year-old is more mature than you."

McENROE ON CONNORS:

"No one could be more phony."

While rivals John McEnroe and Bjorn Borg have contrasting temperaments, the two lefthanders McEnroe and Jimmy Connors are both explosive personalities.

These rivals truly disliked one another, and it spilled over onto the court. McEnroe's dismantling of Connors in the 1984 Wimbledon final was among the most one-sided displays in modern tennis championship history.

The McEnroe–Borg rivalry often went through Connors first, creating a love triangle of sorts for tennis fans. McEnroe and Connors played nine times in Grand Slam tournaments—seven times in the semifinal round—and McEnroe eliminated his nemesis six times.

"Connors, Borg, and McEnroe were tennis's equivalent of Arnold Palmer, Jack Nicklaus, and Gary Player," said tennis analyst Cliff Drysdale. "They captured more millions of viewers and public attention than previous generations of players had ever dreamed possible."

more racket as he was repeatedly warned and often penalized by referees for cursing at linesmen and fined by tournament officials for antagonizing spectators and berating courtside cameramen. In the semifinal match against Rod Frawley his objectionable language caused such a stir that Lady Diana Spencer (soon to become Princess Di) stormed out of the Royal Box, her innocence barely intact.

It had been a tumultuous two weeks for McEnroe, whose agonizing pouts and pained facial expressions prompted the Fleet Street headline makers at the *Sun* to dub him "Super Brat." Most amazing was how he remained focused for the final against Borg despite the commotion. During a crucial moment in the third set, a penetrating McEnroe volley was called good by the baselines judge but the chair umpire overruled the call, leaving McEnroe with two set points against him. He stewed, he seethed, and he steamed, but he kept his head and won those important points.

His side-winding, left-handed serve was the difference in the match, and he used that clutch and effective weapon in both tiebreakers, which he dominated by scores of 7–1 and 7–4. In the tenth game of the fourth set, McEnroe seized his first Wimbledon championship point ever by hitting an overhead for the winner. At the moment of victory McEnroe started to fall to his knees, but perhaps realizing that was exactly how Borg had celebrated for the past five years, instead he briefly flexed his knees and began pumping his fists in the air. It had taken six years, with Borg winning 41 straight matches, for the conqueror to become the conquered.

Tennis observers noted prior to the 1981 U.S. Open that history might not consider Borg one of the best ever unless and until he won the U.S. title. Borg conceded that winning the Open remained his primary ambition, but when a reporter asked if failure to do so would forever be a disappointment, his tone was defensive. "I'm not crying every day if I don't win it," Borg said.

"This is the only place where he's put so much pressure on himself," said McEnroe.

McEnroe foiled the Swede in 1981 and won his third straight U.S. Open title. No player since the legendary Bill Tilden (1920–25) had won three straight national crowns. After splitting the first two sets, McEnroe finished out the third set with a flourish, holding serve at love in the ninth game and breaking Borg in the

THE KING OF ENGLAND: John McEnroe celebrates, but avoids dropping to his knees, after his win at the 1981 Wimbledon tournament. Final score: 4–6, 7–6, 7–6, 6–4.

tenth game for the set.

"That's one of the best games I've played on someone else's serve in a long time," said McEnroe. "Suddenly I felt I could hit just about any shot."

McEnroe was figuring Borg out, and Borg knew it. Using the most delicate of offensive weapons, the forehand topspin lob, McEnroe won several crucial points in the deciding set.

With a fury, McEnroe demolished Borg in the fourth set, again depriving the Swede of his dream of a U.S. Open title. Borg had now lost three major championship finals in a row to McEnroe. Immediately after the loss, a despondent Borg went right from the court to the locker room, skipping the traditional awards ceremony and the postmatch news conference, showering quickly and ducking out a back stairway.

Fifteen months later, in January 1983, Borg retired from the professional tennis circuit, stunning the sports establishment with his announcement that, at 26, he no longer had the motivation to regain the world's No. 1 ranking.

"I cannot give 100 percent," he said, "and if I cannot do that, it would not be fair to myself to go on. Tennis has to be fun if you are to get to the top, and I don't feel that way anymore. That's why I quit."

Borg won six French and five-straight Wimbledon titles, yet would retire without a victory in four U.S. Open finals. In addition to the ascendance of McEnroe, the fact that Borg came so close so often and still failed at the Open undoubtedly affected his confidence. When learning that Borg had quit, one imagines McEnroe uttering for the first time his now signature expression: "You cannot be serious!"

—D.F.

REDSKINS *vs.* COWBOYS

SAY THE WORDS "REDSKINS–COWBOYS" (OR "COWBOYS–REDSKINS," DEPENDING ON WHERE YOU ARE) TO AN NFL FAN, and they'll immediately conjure up images of one of football's fiercest rivalries, filled with tight games, personal rancor, and all the intensity that make for a lasting rivalry. However, the pro football world would have little noted nor likely would have long remembered the rivalry between the Dallas Cowboys and the Washington Redskins based on the happenings of its first decade (1960–1970). That is, not much exciting happened, although the two were in the same division from Dallas's first NFL season in 1960.

And then two things happened. In 1971 George Allen was hired to coach the Redskins. And the Cowboys began calling themselves "America's Team," a display of hubris that did not sit well with many . . . least of all Allen.

NO ONE'S COMPETITIVE FIRE burned brighter than Allen's, who loved to establish battle lines; it made the "us-against-them" factor crystal clear. Allen chose the Cowboys as his team's nemesis because he saw them as the organization that stood between his Redskins and division and conference supremacy (something that had eluded the proud Washington franchise since 1945). When you're picking an enemy, pick the best, and the Cowboys had won five straight division titles heading into Allen's first year.

Allen also relished every contrast between his team and the one from Texas, beginning, of course, with the one between his own emotional self and the cold monolith of Dallas coach Tom Landry. In addition, the Cowboys' quarterback was Roger Staubach, ramrod tall, stainless steel, zero body fat, a luxury sedan of a player. The Redskins' quarterback was Billy Kilmer,

slump-shouldered, rust belt, bulges on bulges, a pickup truck of a player.

Landry and the Cowboys used computers to draft players and discover talent. Allen traded draft choices to get reclamation projects. While the Cowboys were called "America's Team," the Redskins were called "The Over-the-Hill Gang."

Perfect. Let the rivalry begin.

And so it did, and not with a whimper but with a big bang. The Redskins, who had lost six consecutive games to the Cowboys in the three years before Allen arrived (including 24– and 34–point humiliations in 1970), stunned Dallas 20–16 on October 3, 1971.

The Redskins, a mostly mediocre team for years, suddenly had a rebirth. And out of the rebirth came the real beginnings of one of the NFL's classic annual home-and-home match-ups.

"No question, the Cowboys and Landry caught my father's passion full on," said Jennifer Allen, a writer and the only daughter of the coach who died in 1990, at 72. "He had great respect for Landry but he turned that respect inward and there was nobody—nobody—he wanted to beat more.

"He was driven by it. In the off-season, he would be out working in our garden at our home in Virginia and he'd pull on a weed and he'd say, 'If I can get this weed out cleanly, we'll beat the Cowboys.' They were always on his mind."

Allen had coached the Los Angeles Rams for five seasons (1966–1970) before moving to Washington. By the time he relocated to the nation's capital, his obsession with all things Texan had already been cemented.

Allen's Rams teams had been 2–0 against the

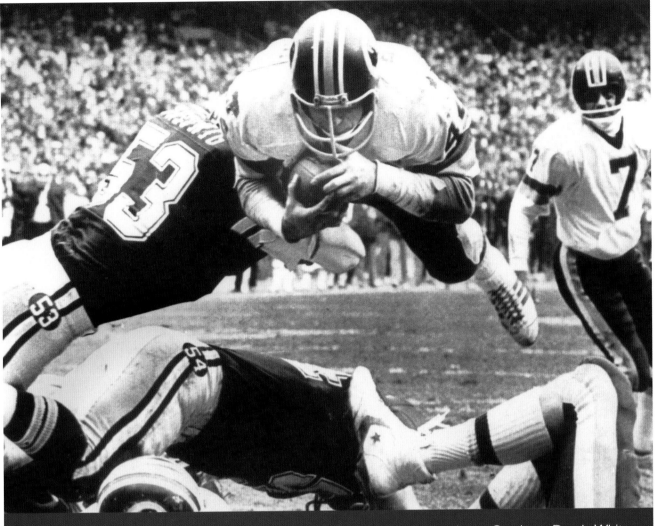

GOING FOR THE GOAL LINE: Redskins running back John Riggins goes up and over Cowboys Randy White and Bob Breunig to score. The Redskins won this NFC Championship Game, 37–17.

Cowboys and Landry. Allen's Redskins teams had a 7–8 record against the Cowboys and Landry, including a 26–3 victory in the 1972 NFC Championship Game.

"We never let up against anyone," said the Redskins' Kilmer, and the numbers offer proof: Allen's Washington teams were 63–25–1 against everyone else. "But every Cowboys game was a grudge match. See, they always had a better-than-you-attitude. Talk about aloof . . . it was very upsetting. And who the hell did they think they were with the America's Team crap?"

Joe Theismann joined the Redskins in 1974, a brainy kid quarterback out of Notre Dame who apprenticed Kilmer for a few seasons.

"Pure and simple, George Allen made this rivalry," Theismann said. "No one else deserves credit.

"He told us we could win a brawl with these guys, that in an old-fashioned, blood-and-guts game, we whip their butts. He used all those words, too . . . and also words like 'running it down their throats' and 'nose bleeds' and how 'we're not gonna be fancy—like them.'"

Theismann laughed softly. "It was darn near 30 years ago but I still get goose bumps. How could you not get motivated? George Allen was the best at it."

Allen and Landry's teams divided regular-season games from 1971–76 (and finished 1–2 in the Eastern Division four of six years) before the Cowboys swept the series in 1977 in what would be Allen's last season. When Allen sought an extended contract for more money, Redskins owner Edward Bennett Williams terminated the relationship.

STAT BOX

FIRST GAME

OCTOBER 9, 1960 • REDSKINS 26–COWBOYS 14

LIFETIME HEAD-TO-HEAD RECORD

COWBOYS 54–REDSKINS 34 (2 TIES)

DIVISION CHAMPIONSHIPS*

* SINCE 1969 AFL-NFL MERGER

REDSKINS: 7

1972, 1982, 1983, 1984, 1987,

1991, 1999

COWBOYS: 15

1970, 1971, 1973, 1976, 1977,

1978, 1979, 1981, 1985, 1992,

1993, 1994, 1995, 1996, 1998

NFL CHAMPIONSHIPS

REDSKINS: 5

1937, 1942, 1982,

1987, 1991

COWBOYS: 5

1971, 1977, 1992,

1993, 1995

BEST AND WORST SEASON RECORD

REDSKINS

BEST: 1983 & 1991 (14-2)

WORST: 1961 (1-12-1)

COWBOYS

BEST: 1992 (13-3)

WORST: 1960 (0-11-1)

A MAN OBSESSED: Redskins coach George Allen talks with his assistant coaches, 1974.

Though the Allen vs. Landry 1970s warfare came to an end, the picture isn't complete without looking at sketches of five games from 1973–76 that helped give Redskins–Cowboys an indelible place on the rivalry map:

•OCTOBER 8, 1973—Washington scored two touchdowns in the final four minutes, then capped a stirring defensive struggle with a goal-line stand in the final minute. Safety Ken Houston's game-saving tackle preserved the victory. Washington 14, Dallas 7.

•NOVEMBER 17, 1974—In a first half of near perfection, the Redskins took a 28–0 lead. The Cowboys proved turnabout is fair play with 21 unanswered second-half points and were threatening to tie the score when a heroic goal-line stand left them short of the end zone as the game ended. Washington 28, Dallas 21.

•NOVEMBER 28, 1974—On Thanksgiving Day, just 11 days after the previous game, rookie quarterback Clint Longley, filling in for injured Roger Staubach, threw a touchdown pass with 35 seconds left to play. Dallas 24, Washington 23.

•NOVEMBER 2, 1975—Bill Kilmer, who passed for 301 yards, sneaked six inches for the winning touchdown in a dramatic overtime thriller. Washington 30, Dallas 24.

•DECEMBER 12, 1976—The Redskins rallied for two late touchdowns to overcome a big day by Roger Staubach and wrap up a spot in the NFL playoffs for the fifth time in George Allen's six years there. Washington 27, Dallas 14.

Lose or win, Staubach was the thorn in the Redskins' side throughout the seventies—and this was despite the best trash-talking, play-stalking efforts of Washington tackle Diron Talbert.

Years later, when Jennifer Allen met Staubach for the first time, she smiled and said, "I used to love to hate you."

He smiled and said, "It was quite a rivalry, wasn't it?" They shook hands and hugged.

But that wasn't the only time Staubach cast warm feelings on the old rivalry. George Allen's favorite food—win or lose but mostly win, of course—was vanilla ice cream. After Allen died, Staubach sent Jennifer, her mother Etty, and the Allen family a literal freezer full of vanilla ice cream.

THOUGH GEORGE ALLEN fathered this rivalry, Redskins' coach Joe Gibbs picked it up in 1981 and, for 12 years, pushed it through adolescence and into adulthood.

Gibbs, like Allen, Landry, and Staubach, a member of the Pro Football Hall of Fame, has some Cowboy classics on his resume, but his record with Dallas doesn't stack up to the rest of his career. Gibbs won three Super Bowls (XVII, XXII, and XXVI) and lost another (XVIII), and had an impressive 128–53 record against the rest of the NFL. However, good as he and his teams were, he was only 12–12 in games against the Cowboys from 1981–1992. An indelible Cowboy half-dozen from the first Gibbs era:

•SEPTEMBER 5, 1983—In a sensational season opener in Washington, the Cowboys overcame the Redskins' 23–3 halftime lead to defeat the defending Super Bowl XVII champions. Dallas 31, Washington 30.
•DECEMBER 9, 1984—The Redskins overcame a 15-point halftime deficit, then got the winning points on a 32-yard interception by Darrell Green. Washington 30, Dallas 28.
•DECEMBER 13, 1987—In a game of memorable hits and defensive stands, the Redskins built a 24–3 lead, then had to hold off a furious Cowboys comeback. Washington 24, Dallas 23.
•SEPTEMBER 9, 1991—Another opening-day masterpiece: The Redskins held off the best of Troy Aikman and Emmitt Smith and penetrated a solid Cowboys defense in an epic battle in Texas. Washington 33, Dallas 31.
•NOVEMBER 24, 1991—The Redskins (who would go on to win Super Bowl XXVI) had visions of an unbeaten season dashed by Cowboys coach Jimmy Johnson's aggressive game plan, which included successful onside kicks and Hail Mary pass plays. Dallas 24, Washington 21.
•DECEMBER 13, 1992—In what would be the last game of his tenure in Washington, Gibbs' team outfought Johnson's team (the latter would win Super Bowl XXVII the following month). Washington 20, Dallas 17.

GIBBS RETIRED AFTER the 1992 season (though he returned in 2004), and Johnson left the Cowboys after the 1993

LUXURY SEDAN PLAYER: Cowboy quarterback Roger Staubach scrambles for a first down, 1975.

season . . . and the rivalry between the Redskins and the Cowboys fell into a state of disrepair.

Without George Allen to pull weeds from his garden and give locker-room speeches for the ages, without Joe Gibbs' brainy game plans, the D.C.–Texas flame has dimmed a bit.

Dallas has won 14 of the last 15 games and is 18–6 since 1992. Added to its superiority in the mid- and late-1960s, the Cowboys lead the overall series 54–34–2.

No two teams have opposed each other more on Monday Night Football than these two. The Cowboys have won seven of the 13 prime-time games. Nine games were decided by seven or less points.

Monday nights aside, maybe it's time to relight the pilot light. Maybe it's time to stop being so overly polite and start showing some real Attitude. Maybe it's time for some blood and guts.

—JOHN WIEBUSCH

Versus

OPPOSITES ATTRACT

REDSKINS	COWBOYS
COACH ALLEN: EMOTIONAL, EXPRESSIVE	COACH LANDRY: COLD, EXPRESSIONLESS
POWERFUL GROUND GAME	PASS-ORIENTED "FLEX" OFFENSE
EAST COAST ESTABLISHMENT WING TIPS	SOUTHWESTERN STYLE COWBOY BOOTS
"HAIL TO THE REDSKINS"	"GO YOU DALLAS COWBOYS GO!"
QB KILMER: SLUMP-SHOULDERED PICKUP TRUCK OF A PLAYER	QB STAUBACH: RAMROD TALL LUXURY SEDAN OF A PLAYER
TRADED DRAFT CHOICES TO GET RECLAMATION PROJECTS	USED COMPUTERS FOR DRAFT
"OVER-THE-HILL GANG"	"AMERICA'S TEAM"

SEABISCUIT vs. WAR ADMIRAL

IN 1938 THE MOST POPULAR ATHLETE IN THE LAND DIDN'T PLAY BASEBALL OR FOOTBALL. HE WASN'T A BOXER, AND HE didn't shoot hoops. The most popular personality in sports that year—and by some measures, the most well known and well covered subject in American newspapers—walked on four legs and ate oats.

That year, thoroughbred champion Seabiscuit became a national hero at five years old, when most racehorses are well past their prime. (He became a hero again in 2001 after the smash success of author Laura Hillenbrand's book *Seabiscuit: An American Legend,* which was followed two years later by the Oscar-nominated movie.) The undersized, crooked-legged horse was the people's favorite to begin with because he had the heart and the will to overcome steep odds. Then his much-awaited, head-to-head match-up with gallant champion War Admiral enthralled a nation still looking for heroes as it overcame the Great Depression.

Seabiscuit was bred at Kentucky's venerable Wheatley Stable and was a plain-looking runt of a thoroughbred with poor racing potential by all appearances, but he had the bloodlines of a champion. In fact, both Seabiscuit and his most famous rival were related to the great champion Man O' War: War Admiral a son, and Seabiscuit a grandson.

Seabiscuit raced for the first time as a juvenile on January 19, 1935, going off as a 17-to-1 long shot (though he finished a respectable fourth). But his handlers were not enamored of the horse's stubborn nature and labeled the two-year-old as lazy. After a busy season that saw him race an amazing 35 times at 11 different tracks, Seabiscuit was virtually discarded to the scrap heap. That's when wealthy San Francisco car dealer Charles S. Howard bought Seabiscuit from the Wheatley Stable for $8,500 in August 1936. Howard installed "Silent" Tom Smith as the trainer, and the trio would prove to be a match made in horseracing heaven.

To ride Seabiscuit, Smith hired a washed-up, blind-in-one eye former prizefighter named Red Pollard, and the fortunes of both jockey and horse immediately changed. Pollard and the 'Biscuit forged a tight bond off the track that is rare between a jockey and his horse. Perhaps because they shared a common underdog persona, the team blossomed. In 1937 Seabiscuit and Pollard won 11 of 15 starts, setting speed records at four different tracks and finishing the year as the top money winner with $168,580 in purses. The horse that had started off slowly was now turning it on.

The other half of this equine rivalry, War Admiral, would become the most decorated son of the legendary Man O' War (Man O' War's only career loss, by the way, came to an opponent called Upset—and yes, that's where the term comes from). In 1936 War Admiral won the first two races he started. A stunning animal, he walked with purposeful, graceful strides and galloped so symmetrically he earned the nickname "The Bay Dancer." War Admiral raced four more times as a two-year-old, earning one victory, two seconds, and a third. But the next year, 1937, no horse could beat him.

As a three-year-old, War Admiral won all eight races he entered, including the Triple Crown; he was only the fourth horse ever to accomplish the feat of capturing in succession the Kentucky Derby, the Preakness Stakes, and the Belmont Stakes. War Admiral was deservedly named Horse of the Year, but he had to share the limelight with another great horse; Seabiscuit, now four years old, was thrilling the nation's sports fans with his rags-to-riches story. Fans clamored for the pair to race against each other, and another kind of race began—the race to match them up.

Match races, featuring one man's horse against another man's horse, were popular contests during thoroughbred racing's golden age. Officials at Belmont Park staked $100,000 (a huge amount in those days) on a match race between the two horses in the fall of 1937, but bad weather postponed the meeting. Then at Santa Anita in February 1938, Pollard was thrown while riding another horse, and his chest was trampled. One of Pollard's lungs collapsed, and as he laid in an intensive care hospital bed it was clear his career as a jockey was over. During his recovery, Pollard convinced Howard to hire his friend and fellow jockey George "Iceman" Woolf to replace him in Seabiscuit's saddle.

Fans awaiting the big race would continue to be disappointed. In May, Seabiscuit had to be withdrawn the day of the race at Suffolk Downs after pulling up lame during a practice run. Arlington Park in Chicago offered $100,000 to the two superstars to race in July, but both owners felt the hot and humid Midwestern weather was not conducive to their mounts and called off the match.

Finally, with the 1938 racing season drawing to a close, one final chance to stage this much-anticipated race was arranged by Alfred Gwynne Vanderbilt Jr., son of the railroad baron, at Pimlico Race Course in Baltimore, Maryland. The winner-take-all purse of $15,000

was far less than the huge sums that were offered for the earlier aborted duels, but being true sportsmen, Howard and War Admiral owner Samuel D. Riddle were more interested in proving whose horse was best; the dollar amount in the pot was secondary.

Finally, on November 1, 1938, the Seabiscuit versus War Admiral dream match-up was about to unfold. A huge crowd of 40,000 showed up, the largest in Pimlico history, to be able to watch in person. For the first time ever, track officials opened the infield to spectators to alleviate the crunch. An estimated forty million fans listened to the race on radio.

Post time for the race was four o'clock, and as the two champions walked from the paddock to the track, War Admiral was the heavy favorite at 1-to-4 while Seabiscuit was the underdog at 2-to-1. Charlie Kurtsinger was aboard War Admiral, while Woolf remained on 'Biscuit as Pollard's replacement. The horses and jockeys prepared for the start. Instead of the normal starting gate, the race would begin using a walking start, a concession to War Admiral's problem with stall starts. After two false starts, the flag dropped a third time and the two horses were on their way. The race was on.

Seabiscuit shot to the lead like a cannon, quickly taking the rail from War Admiral and jumping out to a two-length lead. War Admiral surged forward with his long strides and caught the five-year-old at the far turn, but Seabiscuit refused to let the brown colt pass. By the half-mile mark they were running head-to-head, and

THOROUGHBRED UNDERDOG: Johnny "Red" Pollard sits atop Seabiscuit (left) before the Yonkers Handicap, 1937. Jockey Charles Kurtsinger astride War Admiral (right), 1937.

STAT BOX

SEABISCUIT

BORN: 1933

FIRST RACE: JANUARY 19, 1935 (FINISHED FOURTH)

LIFETIME RECORD: 33 WINS IN 89 RACES

LIFETIME PURSE WINNINGS: $437,730

YEARS RACED: 1935-1940

1935: 35 STARTS, 5 WINS, 12 PLACES

1936: 23 STARTS, 9 WINS, 6 PLACES

1937: 15 STARTS, 11 WINS, 3 PLACES

1938: 11 STARTS, 6 WINS, 5 PLACES

1939: 1 START, 1 PLACE

1940: 4 STARTS, 2 WINS, 1 PLACE

WAR ADMIRAL

BORN: 1934

FIRST RACE: APRIL 25, 1936 (WON)

LIFETIME RECORD: 21 WINS IN 26 RACES

LIFETIME PURSE WINNINGS: $273,240

YEARS RACED: 1936-1939

1936: 6 STARTS, 3 WINS, 3 PLACES

1937: 8 STARTS, 8 WINS

1938: 11 STARTS, 9 WINS, 1 PLACE

1939: 1 START, 1 WIN

ONE SHOT: Seabiscuit leads War Admiral on the first turn during the rivals' sole match-up at Pimlico, 1938.

as they raced through the backstretch neither horse could pull away. Both jockeys were whipping furiously and at the mile marker they were still deadlocked, setting the stage for an exciting finish.

The race would come down to the final ³/₁₆ of a mile—and to which horse had the bigger heart. Would it be the Triple Crown winner, or would it be, as sportswriter Grantland Rice put it, "the horse from the wrong side of the track?" The horses were neck-and-neck around the final turn, but War Admiral, having exhausted himself catching up, was beginning to surrender in mid-stretch. Now there was but one furlong to go, and the crowd gasped as Seabiscuit began pulling ahead. The son of Man O' War was running out of gas while the grandson reached for his reserve and ran harder. Seabiscuit won by three lengths. War Admiral was tiring, so had they gone farther, the margin would have been greater. Seabiscuit won in a track record of 1:56.6, and as the crowd flooded onto the track to congratulate him, jockey Woolf said, "He's the best horse in the world. He proved that today." The trainer Smith, when asked for a statement, declared: "I said mine on the track!"

Despite being a Triple Crown winner and Horse of the Year in 1937, there is no doubt that War Admiral is most famous for one race he lost. Fittingly, both Seabiscuit, named Horse of the Year for 1938, and War Admiral were inducted together into the Hall of Fame at the National Museum of Racing in Saratoga Springs, New York, in 1958.

According to Hillenbrand, Seabiscuit was horse racing's greatest ambassador. "In the latter half of the Depression," she wrote, "Seabiscuit was nothing short of a cultural icon in America, enjoying adulation so intense, it transcended sport." But without a rival like War Admiral to match his skills against, 'Biscuit might never have become the legend he is today.

—D.F.

★ 171 ★

THE ICE WARS
DEBI THOMAS *vs.* KATARINA WITT
MICHELLE KWAN *vs.* IRINA SLUTSKAYA

I N FIGURE SKATING, BEAUTY EQUALS GOLD, AND THUS GOLD IS LITERALLY IN THE EYES OF THE BEHOLDERS—THE JUDGES. Great skaters face off as much against the judges as each other. They skate one after the other in a constant game of one-upsmanship, with their skills on the ice meshing in judges' minds with the reputation that each brings into the competition.

Thus the battles on the ice are just part of the often chilly show that is top-level international figure skating. It's more than just who does the perfect routine, who lands the most difficult jumps, it can often be about who charms the judges, who has built the reputation that will pay off in points. And underneath their painted smiles, their sequined costumes, and their buoyant on-ice personalities, top female figure skaters are competing with their rivals as fiercely as in any sport.

Two pairs of skaters of recent decades crystallize this combination of on-ice/off-ice rivalry. They also offer a look at how changing world politics can affect perception in sports.

In 1986 a Stanford premed student named Debi Thomas, after long and hard work through her teen years, reached the peak of her sport, winning first the United States and then the world championship. Thomas was a trailblazer of sorts, the first African-American to win either of those titles. She learned about adversity when, earlier in her career, she saw blond teen pixies fail to match her own complicated, athletic routines and yet win in the eyes of judges. Overcoming this unspoken bias was a mission for her, but she didn't let it get in the way of her quest for the top titles.

At the '86 Worlds, her main competition was a stunning beauty from East Germany, Katarina Witt. In a world of smallish skaters doing outlandish leaps, Witt was a graceful tall swan pirouetting into the hearts of fans. Not only was she an outstanding skater, she was model-beautiful and the then-Communist East Germans trotted her out as another example of their supposed superiority. She was called the "worker's hero" and called herself a "diplomat in warm-ups."

In 1988 she told *TIME* magazine, "When I do well, coming from a socialist country, other countries have grounds to respect us."

Thomas came into the 1986 Worlds as the unexpected United States champ, and her odds for another win weren't expected to be great. But she completely out-skated the favored Witt, who had won the previous two world titles . . . and would win the two following Thomas's win.

AT THE GAMES IN CALGARY, ANOTHER BATTLE BETWEEN EAST AND WEST WAS JOINED, BETWEEN EAST GERMANY'S FUTURE ACTRESS AND AMERICA'S FUTURE DOCTOR.

YEAH, YOU BETTER LOOK THE OTHER WAY: Debi Thomas (left) and Katarina Witt avoid each other before a Calgary Olympics practice session.

Injuries kept Thomas from repeating her feat in 1987, but she once again beat the odds in 1988, an Olympic year. At the Games in Calgary, another battle between East and West was joined, between East Germany's future actress and America's future doctor. As Thomas looked ahead to the competition in Calgary, she said, "I'll get there and I'll love it. One moment of glory is worth everything."

At the Games in Calgary, an unusual coincidence made the match-up between the two even more pronounced. Both skaters chose to perform their final programs to music from *Carmen*, the opera by Bizét. Both skaters did well in the preliminary rounds, and the finals were watched anxiously by millions on both sides of the Iron Curtain. In the end, though Thomas

skated well, she did not reach perfection. Witt did, and combined with her stunning grace and high-wattage smile, it was enough to win gold. Thomas came in third, behind Canada's Elizabeth Manley, and her skating career ended shortly thereafter. East Germany itself disappeared a year later when the Berlin Wall fell. Under her new flag of Germany, Witt embraced the consumer culture of the West and became the actress and model she wanted to be.

IN RECENT YEARS, another pair of skaters has dueled over and over, continuing their match-ups on the ice even through the 2005 World Championships. Michelle Kwan is perhaps America's most titled skater, having tied a record with nine United States championships,

STAT BOX

KATARINA WITT

BORN: DECEMBER 3, 1965

WORLD CHAMPION:

1984, 1985, 1987, 1988

OLYMPIC GOLD MEDAL:

1984, 1988

EUROPEAN CHAMPION:

1983, 1984, 1985, 1986,

1987, 1988

DEBI THOMAS

BORN: MARCH 25, 1967

WORLD CHAMPION:

1986

WORLD SILVER MEDAL:

1987

OLYMPIC BRONZE MEDAL:

1988

U.S. NATIONAL CHAMPION:

1986, 1988

IRINA SLUTSKAYA

BORN: FEBRUARY 9, 1979

WORLD CHAMPION:

2002, 2005

OLYMPIC SILVER MEDAL:

2002

EUROPEAN CHAMPION:

1996, 1997, 2000, 2001,

2003, 2005

MICHELLE KWAN

BORN: JULY 7, 1980

WORLD CHAMPION:

1996, 1998, 2000, 2001, 2003

OLYMPIC SILVER MEDAL:

1998

OLYMPIC BRONZE MEDAL:

2002

U.S. NATIONAL CHAMPION:

1996, 1998, 1999, 2000, 2001,

2002, 2003, 2004, 2005

ONE MOMENT OF GLORY: Katarina Witt, left, and Debi Thomas in Calgary, 1988. Coincidentally, both competitors performed to music from the opera *Carmen*.

while also winning five world titles. Kwan is the all-American girl, appearing in ads for milk, visiting with school children, and picking up the torch of America's ice princess carried previously by the likes of Peggy Fleming, Dorothy Hamill, and Thomas.

Many skaters have come and gone to challenge her reign as the world's best, but one seems to pop up again and again at big moments to make a run, or should we say a skate, at the American: Russia's Irina Slutskaya. And so the new-millennium version of East vs. West in this international sports battle continues.

The two remember well their first meeting in 1994, Kwan recalling her rival's odd ballerina-like tutu and lucky stuffed animal, Slutskaya reminiscing that Kwan was amazed to see the Russian wearing black skates.

While Kwan has dominated United States championships, Slutskaya has won six European titles. She

also defeated Kwan in nine other important competitions from 2000 to 2004. However, Slutskaya has only rarely been able to overcome her big rival at the World Championships, finishing second to Kwan on three occasions and third on another. She made a breakthrough in 2002, however, finally earning her first world title, with Kwan second.

At the Salt Lake City Games in 2002, the rivalry between the two continued on center stage leading up to the competition. Although she had created an impressive resume, Kwan had never won an Olympic gold medal, with a best finish of second in 1998. At 21, though certainly no greybeard, most observers felt she was probably heading toward the end of her effective years. She had been a world-class skater for more than eight years, a long time in an intense sport. And she had lost earlier that winter to Slutskaya at the Worlds.

DOUBLE CHOKE: Michelle Kwan, left, and Irina Slutskaya in Salt Lake City, 2002. Both stumbled leading up to the gold, and neither took it home.

SLUTSKAYA SKATED NEAR THE END OF THE ROUND AND PUT UP A DAZZLING PROGRAM. THEN KWAN WENT OUT AND JUST DID BETTER.

The two were the clear leaders as the preliminary round went on. Slutskaya skated near the end of the round and put up a dazzling program, filled with the athletic spins for which she is best known. Then Kwan went out and just did better. "I felt loose, I felt calm, I felt America behind me," the California native said. "I skated from my heart tonight and I had fun."

"I am ready," Slutskaya answered. "I will fight."

Remarkably, after the final free skate a few nights later, neither skater stood in the top spot on the medal stand. Both had inexplicably and unexpectedly stumbled, leaving the door open for young American Sarah Hughes to explode onto the world scene with a breathtaking performance. Slutskaya held on to second, but Kwan dropped to third. Irina had beaten her rival, but ended up losing.

Did Kwan and Slutskaya focus too much on each other and forget the rest of the field? In rivalries like these, blinders to the fact that the field is more than one opponent can lead to disaster.

Still, Kwan's place in history is secure, thanks to her many other titles. Perhaps her greatest rivals have been herself, as she continues to battle for an elusive Olympic gold and history, as she continues to chase several all-time marks for championships. She added two more United States titles after her 2002 disappointment.

The rivalry continued, and at the 2005 World Championships all eyes, including each other's, were on the pair. But the gaze was friendlier.

"We got to know each other more after 2002," Kwan told the *Los Angeles Times* leading up to the '05 contest. "We got a chance to talk [during post-Olympics skating tours]. It's a friendly rivalry, and in skating, that's very unusual."

"[Kwan] is a great skater and a great competitor," Slutskaya said in the same article. "I am happy to compete with her for a long time. I think we both [have grown] stronger and into powerful and smart girls."

Kwan had competed only sporadically entering the event, reducing her schedule to maintain top form for the big competitions. Whereas Slutskaya, though still recovering from an inflammation that affected her heart, came in hot, having won six recent competitions.

Kwan fell, literally and figuratively, while Slutskaya soared. All the skaters were judged under a new system that awarded points to various technical elements. Kwan's program didn't measure up, and a fall in the short program also cost her points. Fifth after the preliminaries, she couldn't catch up. Slutskaya, on the other hand, triumphed, leading after all three rounds. She showed serious guts, overcoming the fatigue caused by her condition (called vasculitis) and won her second world title. Kwan finished fourth.

Next stop for this rivalry will probably be the 2006 Winter Olympics in Turin, Italy. Neither owns the one piece of championship hardware they each seek most: an Olympic gold medal.

—J.B.

SPORTS KNOW-IT-ALL

WHERE ARE THEY NOW?

THOMAS

- Earned degrees in engineering and later doctorate in medicine.
- Mother of Christopher, born in 1999.
- Elected to International Skating Hall of Fame.
- Holds skating clinics for youngsters.
- Served on national committees for United States Skating Sports Medicine and United States Olympic Sports Medicine Committees.

WITT

- After leaving competitive skating, starred in numerous ice shows.
- Acted in several movies, including Robert de Niro film *Ronin*.
- Won an Emmy for work in *Carmen on Ice*, a 1990 HBO special.
- Has worked as color commentator for several networks at international ice competitions.
- In 1993 was first German athlete to win the Jim Thorpe Pro Sports Award for contributions on and off the ice.
- Runs international sports marketing company.

MIKE TYSON *vs.* EVANDER HOLYFIELD

MOST OF THE RIVALRIES IN THIS BOOK ARE PACKED WITH PIVOTAL MOMENTS. THE FACE-OFFS OFFER UP MANY GREAT memories, events that act as symbols of the long rivalry or call to mind particular players or specific games. But when one thinks of the battles between heavyweight boxers Evander Holyfield and Mike Tyson, there's really only one moment.

When Tyson bit off the top of Holyfield's ear.

However, that moment, probably the most shocking in boxing history and certainly among the most bizarre in all of sports history, had some great stories leading up to it, stories and moments and memories lost in the blood, gore, and spectacle of "Iron Mike" clamping down on Holyfield's right ear, seeming to permanently sever the connection between sanity and the once-lauded young champion from Brooklyn.

Though he has since become almost a caricature of himself, tattooed and convicted and parodied, at one point Mike Tyson was probably the most feared and among the most famous people on the planet. When he came up in the early 1980s, the fight game was in a downslide. Since the end of Muhammad Ali's effective career in the late 1970s (he continued to box into the early 1980s, but without the splendor of his younger days), the heavyweight ranks had divided into warring world councils, organizations, and associations. The once-vaunted title of "undisputed heavyweight champ" had been diluted by the proliferations of pretenders to that throne who had claimed one of a number of world "belts."

Into this mix stalked a bull-headed 18-year-old who wore severe plain black shorts, plain black boots, and an expression of pure hate toward anyone who faced him. Raised on the prototypical mean streets, Tyson brought a ferocity and power to the ring that had really never been seen. Fighters had usually mixed in some grace, some poise, a sense of understanding of the separation that the ropes of the ring made from "real life." Even a famous power puncher like Joe Frazier went to church regularly (heck, he later became a singer). But Tyson seemed to step beyond the boundaries of "sport," and sought as much to destroy, to hurt, to kill, as to win. To put it another way, the Marquis of Queensbury never saw Mike Tyson fight.

He quickly caught the public's eye and they watched, fascinated, as he destroyed opponent after opponent. By the age of 20, after only about 30 pro fights, he had become such a dominant personality and talent that he affected a reunification of the titles. He beat all comers, knocked off all challengers. In 1985 and 1986, he won 27 fights, nearly all by knockout and 15 of them in the first round. Then, after beating Tony Tucker in 1987, he was what no one had been for 15 years: the undisputed heavyweight champion of the world.

MANY FELT THAT HOLYFIELD'S CAREER WOULD NOT BE COMPLETE WITHOUT FACING—AND DEFEATING—TYSON.

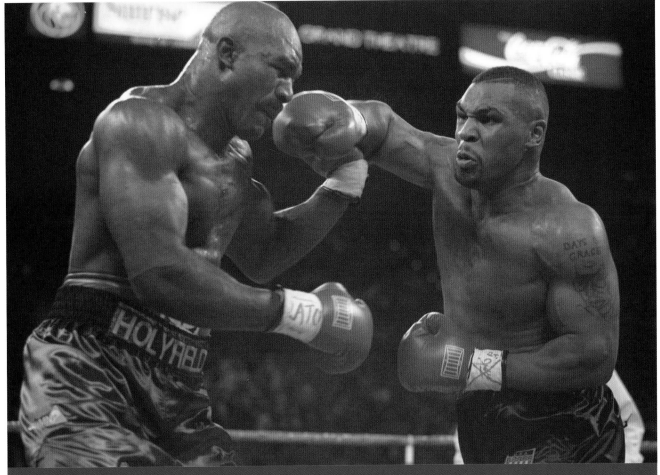

ANGRY MAN: Mike Tyson throws a right hook at Evander Holyfield during their first fight at the MGM Grand Garden in Las Vegas, 1996.

For the next three-plus years, he held the crown and the stunned eyes of the sports world. He beat Leon Spinks in 1987 in 91 seconds to earn $20 million. In 1988 he beat Leon's brother Michael in just about the same amount of time. Though events such as his marriage to Robin Givens somewhat softened the tough kid from Brownsville, Tyson's rage seemed ever ready to surface. His name was in the papers more for his scuffles away from the ring than for his pugilism in it.

His reign came to a sudden and decisive end in 1990, when he was upset by a happy-go-lucky Buster Douglas, whose sunny demeanor seemed to counteract Tyson's anger. All of a sudden, the heavyweight world was again in turmoil. Tyson seemed to wander aimlessly for a while, and dangerously. In 1992, seemingly lining up to try to regain his crown, he was convicted of rape in Indiana and spent the next three years in prison. Released in 1995, he knew he had to find his way back to the ring.

Opposing him would be an individual who was Tyson's opposite in many ways. Evander Holyfield was a devoutly religious man, a clean-living role model to young men, and a devastating boxer as an athlete. His first words after a fight were to thank God for giving him strength. (Before facing the famously fearsome Tyson, Holyfield said, "I'm led by the Holy Spirit, so whatever I do, I know I will have enough to win.") While Tyson would later boast that he wished to "eat the children" of an opponent, Holyfield was quoted as saying, "I don't have nothin' but love for people."

Holyfield had become the top boxer in the land while Tyson was away, first capturing the heavyweight title himself in 1991 by defeating Douglas. He lost the undisputed title to Riddick Bowe in 1992 and announced his "retirement." But he came back to the

STAT BOX

TYSON–HOLYFIELD I

DATE: NOVEMBER 9, 1996

SITE: LAS VEGAS, NEVADA

TYSON: 222 POUNDS

HOLYFIELD: 215 POUNDS

ODDS: TYSON FAVORED 16–1

WINNER: HOLYFIELD IN AN 11-ROUND TKO

TYSON–HOLYFIELD II

DATE: JUNE 28, 1997

SITE: LAS VEGAS, NEVADA

TYSON: 218 POUNDS

HOLYFIELD: 218 POUNDS

ODDS: TYSON FAVORED 2–1

WINNER: HOLYFIELD BY DISQUALIFICATION AT THE END

OF THE 3RD

CAREER OVERALL RECORDS

TYSON A.K.A. "IRON MIKE"

- 50 WINS (44 BY KNOCKOUT)

- 5 LOSSES

- 0 DRAWS

- UNDISPUTED WORLD CHAMPION

  AUGUST 1987–FEBRUARY 1990

HOLYFIELD: A.K.A. THE "REAL DEAL"

- 38 WINS (25 BY KNOCKOUT)

- 8 LOSSES

- 2 DRAWS

- UNDISPUTED WORLD CHAMPION

  OCTOBER 1990–NOVEMBER 1992

TIT FOR TAT: Evander Holyfield punches Mike Tyson as their first fight wears on. Holyfield was the victor, paving the way for a bizarre and historic rematch.

ring, retiring again after losing WBA and International Boxing Federation titles to Michael Mooer in 1995. However, when Tyson was let back out into the world, the prospect of facing the younger fighter was too much to ignore. Many felt that Holyfield's career would not be complete without facing—and defeating—Tyson.

The two personalities created a clash of cultures that made their first bout an enormous draw. Their first fight was on November 10, 1996, with Tyson the huge betting favorite. Though his four tune-up fights after his release from prison had not shown his old power and tenacity, Tyson remained a feared presence. To this point, he had fought 46 times and lost only once (to Douglas). He had knocked out 39 of his opponents.

Holyfield started as a 25–1 underdog to Tyson. It wasn't even that close—but in the direction opposite of that expected by bettors. Ignoring the odds, Holyfield took the fight to Tyson, and the younger man couldn't

keep it up. Holyfield also never let the famously powerful inside fighting style of Tyson succeed, tying up Tyson's arms or counterpunching ferociously. In the sixth, he knocked Tyson down with a left hook. It was only the second time in his life Tyson had hit the canvas in a fight. By the 11th, Holyfield was hitting Tyson almost unopposed. A 12–punch series was stopped by the referee and it was over. Holyfield had knocked off the "most dangerous man on earth." With it came the World Boxing Association championship, making Holyfield only the second boxer since Muhammad Ali to regain a heavyweight crown he had lost.

Of course, this being boxing, the obvious next move: set the date for the rematch.

Fight fans didn't have to wait long. Just over six months later, in June 1997, the two men met again. Again the fight was enormously hyped, and again the prefight publicity showcased the startling differences between the two fighters. Holyfield continued with

DISQUALIFIED: Holyfield holds his ear after Tyson bit it during their 1997 fight.

his prayerful yet determined stance, while Tyson met reporters with parts of his life story: "I've been abused. I've been dehumanized. I've been humiliated."

Each fighter was guaranteed at least $30 million for the fight. It was seen by a packed house at the MGM Grand in Las Vegas and by millions more on pay-per-view worldwide. Everyone who saw the event will long remember it.

Holyfield started out strongly and led on all the judges' cards after two rounds. In the first round, the two had butted heads, and Tyson looked enraged. Another head butt in the second opened a small cut on Tyson's forehead.

The third round was action-packed to start, with both fighters landing solid blows. In the third minute of the round, the two got in a clinch and then Holyfield pushed backward, grabbing the side of his head.

Tyson had bit his opponent's right ear.

"I couldn't believe it," Holyfield said. Neither could anyone else. The referee pulled the fighter aside and had him examined by a ring doctor. Then the two were brought back to the center to finish the round.

Again they clinched, and, incredibly, Tyson bit Holyfield's ear again, and this time Tyson drew blood . . . and more. The sight of the tip of Holyfield's ear being flung from the mouth of Tyson is one of sport's

THE RING WAS SUDDENLY FILLED WITH A SCRUM OF PEOPLE SHOVING, PUSHING, AND TRYING TO CORRAL TYSON.

A FOUR-WAY
BOXING RIVALRY

Boxing's lower weight divisions are so closely spaced that in some cases a fighter, with a bit of diet or a bit of weight work, can easily move up or down from one to another. In the 1980s, a quartet of outstanding fighters did just that, all the while mixing and matching to create a jigsaw puzzle of boxing rivalries that showcased a wide variety of personal and pugilistic styles. Welterweight and 1976 Olympic gold medalist Sugar Ray Leonard, known as the "pretty" one, used smooth moves, quick jabs, and a slick style. Roberto Duran, a stolid puncher, relied on power and endurance more than points-scoring punching. Leonard was the welterweight champ in 1980 when the two met in Montreal. After a furious toe-to-toe battle, Duran surprised many by winning the 15-round decision. Their rematch is one for the history books. Held at the enormous Louisiana Superdome, Leonard dominated the match. In a real stunner, however, Duran stayed in his corner before the eighth round, his cry of "*No más, no más*" entering the sports vocabulary. Leonard earned the win and a place in boxing history.

Before they fought a third time, each had to deal with the other members of the quartet. Leonard defeated stylish Thomas Hearns to capture all parts of the world welterweight titles. Duran tried to win the slightly heavier middleweight title, but lost to powerful "Marvelous" Marvin Hagler, whose own fights with Hearns had been among boxing's best of the decade. Leonard would come back in 1987 to defeat Hagler. Duran lost to Hearns, meanwhile, while Leonard battled Hearns to a draw in 1989.

In 1989 a lackluster third pairing of Leonard and Duran resulted in a Sugar Ray win in 12 rounds. After a decade of bouts between a quartet of great fighters, this particular boxing merry-go-round rang to a close.

oddest of all time. The man literally bit off the top of his opponent's ear. Blood dripped from his mouth and along the side of Holyfield's face.

"It was the most bizarre thing I've ever seen in boxing," said the referee, Mills Lane, echoing the thoughts of everyone involved with the fiasco.

Holyfield was led to his corner to be treated. Tyson went to his to seethe. Officials conferred and then the decision was announced.

Fight over. Tyson disqualified. Holyfield wins.

Then the real fun started. Tyson charged out after anyone who came in his way. Police poured into the ring

to restore order. The fans were on their feet demanding an explanation. The ring was suddenly filled with a scrum of people shoving, pushing, and trying to corral Tyson, who was, by all appearances, going nuts.

Holyfield went to the hospital to have his ear piece reattached. Tyson went to history, ignominous, feared, shamed, his record of achievement now permanently a footnote to the capper of a life of bizarre behavior.

A memorable moment? That's one way of looking at it.

—J.B.

JEFF GORDON vs. DALE EARNHARDT SR. & JR.

WE END OUR COLLECTION OF GREAT RIVALRIES WITH NOT ONE BUT A PAIR, ONE THAT WAS AND ONE THAT WELL MAY be. One part of the rivalry is tragically past, while the second has an eerie connection to the first. The competition between Jeff Gordon and both Dale Earnhardt Sr. and Jr. also provides a good look at the rapid rise of NASCAR in the past decade, and how the personalities of the sport's drivers remain, well . . . the driving force in creating fan interest.

Dale Earnhardt Sr. was the grim-lipped, black-goggled, mustachioed face of NASCAR in the 1980s. The "Man in Black" combined outstanding racing skills with a take-no-prisoners style on the track. He won his first title in 1980 and would go on to win six more in his storied career to tie the great Richard Petty (see page 104). Though many racers challenged Earnhardt, none really stood the test. His grizzled, gruff approach, while not exactly cereal-box-cover material at first, made him a down-home hero to millions of fans. He was the champ in 1980, 1986, 1987, 1990, and 1991.

Then came the "Kid." Raised in Indiana near the famous Indianapolis Speedway, Jeff Gordon at first thought his destiny was in open-wheel racing. But he found that he was a pretty danged good stock-car driver, reaching the top ranks of NASCAR in 1992 when he was only 21. The 1991 Busch Series rookie of the year made his first Winston Cup start in '92, ironically in the final start of the legendary Petty. There was a palpable sense of passing the torch that helped kick off Gordon's career. "Watch out for that Gordon kid," said the King. "He's the future." The future got his first race win in 1994, and the veterans were clearly taking notice of him. Even Dale Sr. saw the potential, saying in 1993, "I've never seen anyone this good at this age. His talent, his feel for the race car, he'll be good wherever he goes."

Earnhardt Sr. was still the champ, however, and won two more titles in 1993 and 1994. But in 1995 Gordon, the young man that Dale Sr. dubbed "Wonder Boy," arrived at the top. The pair never tangled directly on the track, though they each won a 1–2 race finish that year. The final race of the season was in Atlanta; to clinch the points needed for the crown, Gordon simply had to finish. Earnhardt, to win the title, would have to win the race and lead most of the way, piling up points in an effort to catch the Kid. Earnhardt did his part, winning the race easily, but Gordon did, too, edging Dale Sr. by 34 points to win his first NASCAR championship. In a nascent rivalry, it was fitting that their most important 1–2 finish came in the final season standings.

For his part, Earnhardt, also known as the "Intimidator," was disappointed, as much for the lack of drama as the lack of a championship. "We never really went

"I'VE NEVER SEEN ANYONE THIS GOOD AT THIS AGE" —DALE EARNHARDT SR. ON THE YOUNG JEFF GORDON, 1993

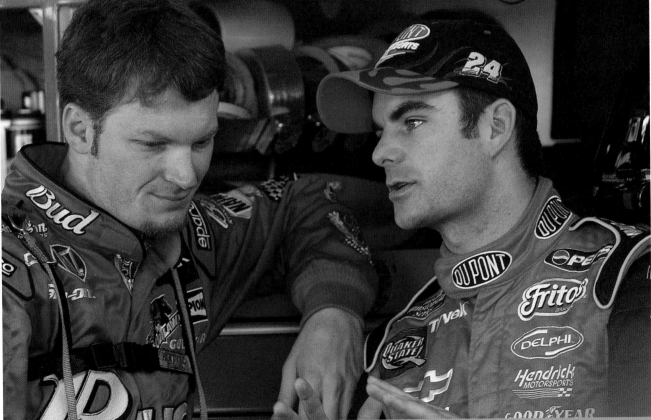

LIKE FATHER, LIKE SON: (Top) Dale Earnhardt Sr., 1997. (Below) Dale Earnhardt Jr. and Jeff Gordon share a few words during a practice for the Pontiac Excitement 400, 2003.

CLOSING IN: Jeff Gordon (#24) and Dale Earnhardt Sr. (#3) fight for the lead during the Cracker Barrel 500 NASCAR Winston Cup Series race, 1999.

fender-to-fender with him and raced down to the wire." In his typical grumbling style, he said Gordon would probably have to drink milk instead of the traditional champagne at the season-ending banquet. On the night of that event in New York, Gordon laughed and toasted his elder . . . with a champagne flute of milk.

Veteran racing observers looked at the pair and harkened back to Petty and David Pearson, or Cale Yarborough and Bobby Allison, and wondered if the duo would become another great rivalry on the track. But Gordon sped way ahead of *any* rivalry after that, winning titles in 1997 and 1998. He was the circuit superstar. Though Earnhardt continued racing, it looked as if his time was past (a highlight was his first Daytona 500 victory in 1998, in his 20th try at NASCAR's biggest race).

Though Gordon pulled ahead, in many senses he brought Earnhardt with him. "It's real simple: 1992," three-time NASCAR champ and popular broadcaster Darrell Waltrip said to *Sports Illustrated* in 2004. "That's the year that Jeff Gordon showed up. When he did, that kind of good guy/bad guy rivalry developed. Jeff started winning a lot of races, and I think fans started to support Earnhardt more because they didn't want to see Gordon win all the races." Dale Sr. took on a veneer of beloved elder statesman, while the Kid continued to create as many enemies as fans. By 1997, Earnhardt became the first race car driver honored on a box of Wheaties—a far cry from the surly Man in Black image.

The pair had one final run at each other, in the 1999 Daytona 500. Gordon got in front late and Earnhardt got on his tail. The pair dueled for the final ten laps, with Earnhardt Sr. trying every

STAT BOX

DALE EARNHARDT, SR.

BORN: APRIL 29, 1951, KANNAPOLIS, NORTH CAROLINA

(DIED FEBRUARY 18, 2001)

OFFICIAL ROOKIE SEASON: 1979 (ROOKIE OF THE YEAR)

STARTS: 676

RACE WINS: 76

NASCAR TITLES: 7 (1980, 1986, 1987, 1990, 1991, 1993, 1994)

DAYTONA 500 WINS: 1 (1998)

JEFF GORDON

BORN: AUGUST 4, 1971, VALLEJO, CALIFORNIA

OFFICIAL ROOKIE SEASON: 1993 (ROOKIE OF THE YEAR)

STARTS: 413 (THROUGH MAY 15, 2005)

RACE WINS: 72 (THROUGH MAY 15, 2005)

NASCAR TITLES: 4 (1995, 1997, 1998, 2001)

DAYTONA 500 WINS: 3 (1997, 1999, 2005)

DALE EARNHARDT, JR.

BORN: OCT. 10, 1974, KANNAPOLIS, NORTH CAROLINA

OFFICIAL ROOKIE SEASON: 2000

STARTS: 195 (THROUGH MAY 15, 2005)

RACE WINS: 15 (THROUGH MAY 15, 2005)

NASCAR TITLES: 0

DAYTONA 500 WINS: 1 (2004)

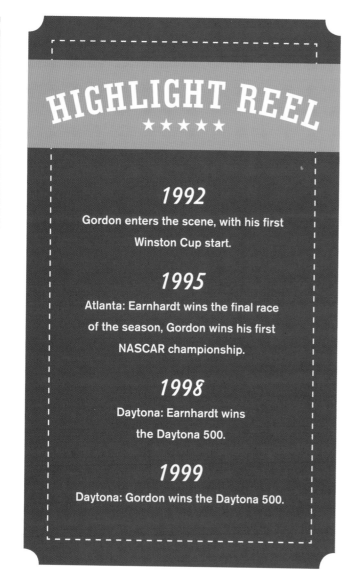

HIGHLIGHT REEL
★ ★ ★ ★ ★

1992

Gordon enters the scene, with his first
Winston Cup start.

1995

Atlanta: Earnhardt wins the final race
of the season, Gordon wins his first
NASCAR championship.

1998

Daytona: Earnhardt wins
the Daytona 500.

1999

Daytona: Gordon wins the Daytona 500.

the guy I learned from. That was the longest ten laps of my life!"

Though Gordon won that race, he never captured the hearts of the fans as Earnhardt Sr. had (and still does!). Gordon was respected, but also hated by many, mostly for having the temerity to challenge the beloved Earnhardt Sr. Guys in black hats always seemed to have a bit of an edge in good ol' NASCAR.

Sadly, when it seemed that the rivalry might enter into the annals as an all-time great, it ended with fatal certainty in the 2001 Daytona 500. Helping to protect teammate Michael Waltrip's lead late in the race, Dale Sr. was clipped from behind, lost control, and smashed headfirst into the outer wall of the famed track. He died almost instantly. The racing world mourned, and, in some ways, still mourns today. (As a mercenary note to that statement: Through 2003, sales of Dale Sr. merchandise trailed those of only three other drivers. One was 2002 champ Tony Stewart. The other two? Gordon and Dale Jr.)

On the track that fateful day was a driver who would continue not only the Earnhardt name, but also the rivalry with Gordon. Dale Earnhardt Jr. was a two-time Busch Series champion who had joined the Winston Cup circuit full-time the year before, winning twice as a rookie. His laidback personal style, in contrast to his dad's perpetual gruffness, combined with the fans' continued love of Dale Sr., made the younger Earnhardt almost instantly the most popular driver in the sport. Fans immediately looked to him to renew the alleged feud with Gordon.

For his part, Gordon continues to drive a Chrysler . . . and dodge the rivalry issue. "You know what I've always said about rivalries. I've always believed that to win a championship, you compete against yourself,

trick in the book to pass the younger driver; for each move the Intimidator made, Gordon had an answer. Earnhardt was fractions of a second behind, about two car lengths, as they passed under the checkered flag.

"Winning this race was much sweeter and more meaningful," Gordon said, "because I was battling

---

"I WOULD LOVE TO COME TO EVERY RACE TRACK AND HAVE IT COME DOWN TO A FIVE-LAP SHOOTOUT BETWEEN ME AND JEFF . . . I DON'T THINK THERE IS ANYBODY ELSE I'D RATHER BEAT"
—DALE EARNHARDT JR., 2004

LOST HERO: A mourner signs a memorial for Dale Earnhardt Sr., 2001.

not really against any one competitor," he said in 2003. "Some weekends it's one guy, the next weekend it's another." Earnhardt Jr. and Gordon were part of the first NASCAR Chase for the Nextel Cup in 2004, when the top ten drivers after 26 races entered a special competition among themselves for the newly renamed trophy (it was the Winston Cup for the previous 31 years). Both men were among the favorites to come out on top; fans clamored for them to turn the top ten into a top two. Junior had no problem playing into the game, much as his old man had done with his needling of young Gordon.

"I would love to come to every race track and have it come down to a five-lap shootout between me and Jeff," Earnhardt said in November 2004. "I don't think there is anybody else I'd rather beat."

But once again, Gordon, this time the elder statesman in the rivalry, played the diplomat, even while recognizing the racing zeitgeist. "I have great respect for Dale [Jr.]," he said. "It's the fans who are more intense. There are Junior fans and Gordon fans, but rarely are they both. I know people would like to see it come down to us because of the popularity. It was the same way with Dale Sr. It's fun."

Gordon's opinion is backed up by the folks in the grandstands and in the mobile home parks that spring up on NASCAR infields every weekend. For both of the Gordon–Earnhardt rivalries, it is the fans who live and breathe the match-up more than the drivers. They are indeed up against 42 other drivers in every race, not just one guy. Sure, they'll bump fenders now and again, and you can bet that Gordon and Junior will find themselves 1–2 at some race in the future. They'll each want to win as much as their fans want them to win.

—J.B.

ABOUT THE AUTHORS

JAMES BUCKLEY JR. has written more than forty books on sports for adults and young readers, including *Perfect: The Story of Baseball's 17 Perfect Games; Baseball: A Celebration; Classic Ballparks;* and *Sports Immortals.* Once a writer and editor for *Sports Illustrated* and NFL Publishing, Buckley now operates the Shoreline Publishing Group, a book producer specializing in sports books. He lives in Santa Barbara, California, with his wife Patty and children Conor and Katie.

DAVID FISCHER is the author of *The New York Times' Sports of the Times; The 50 Coolest Jobs in Sports;* and other titles. He has written for numerous publications, including *Sports Illustrated for Kids* and the *New York Times*, and has worked for NBC Sports, *Sports Illustrated,* and the *National Sports Daily.* He lives in northern New Jersey with his wife Carolyn and children Rachel and Jack.

PHOTO CREDITS

Getty Images

p. 4-5 (left to right, top row to bottom): Al Bello; Steve Powell; Rick Stewart; John Shearer/Time Life Pictures; Danny Moloshok; Craig Jones; Andy Lyons; Tim Defrisco; Henry Groskinsky/Time Life Pictures; Stan Wayman/Time Life Pictures; Karen Levy; Focus on Sport; Focus on Sport; Hy Peskin/Time Life Pictures; Getty; Doug Pensinger; National Baseball Hall of Fame Library/MLB Photos; Bruce Bennett Studios; David Cannon; STF/AFP; Bruce Bennett Studios; Keeneland/Morgan Collection; Jerome Delay/AFP; Al Bello; Robert Laberge.

p. 11: Hulton Archive
p. 13: National Baseball Hall of Fame Library/MLB Photos
p. 14: Photo File
p. 17: Al Bello
p. 19: Rich Pilling/MLB Photos
p. 23: Rich Clarkson/Time Life Pictures
p. 24-25: Rich Clarkson/Time Life Pictures
p. 29: Steve Powell
p. 32: Cornell Capa/Time Life Pictures
p. 35: George Skadding/Time Life Pictures
p. 37: Herb Scharfman/Time Life Pictures
p. 38: Rick Stewart
p. 41: John Shearer/Time Life Pictures
p. 42: John Shearer/Time Life Pictures
p. 44-45: John Shearer/Time Life Pictures
p. 47: Getty
p. 48: Keystone
p. 59: Danny Moloshok
p. 61: Streeter Lecka
p. 63: (left) Rich Clarkson/Time Life Pictures
p. 63: (right) Craig Jones
p. 64: Craig Jones
p. 73: Andy Lyons
p. 76: Bill Ray/Time Life Pictures
p. 79: Tim Defrisco
p. 81: Christian Petersen
p. 83: Henry Groskinsky/Time Life Pictures
p. 84: Kidwiler Collection/Diamond Images
p. 85: Photo File
p. 86: Bruce Bennett Studios
p. 89: Stephen Dunn
p. 91: Stan Wayman/Time Life Pictures
p. 100: George Silk/Time Life Pictures
p. 102: Karen Levy
p. 105: (right) Focus on Sport

p. 111: Focus on Sport
p. 114: Focus on Sport
p. 117: Hy Peskin/Time Life Pictures
p. 120: Andrew D. Bernstein/NBAE
p. 122: Jim Cummins/NBAE
p. 125: Hulton Archive
p. 126: Reg Lancaster/Express
p. 129: Focus on Sport
p. 130: Getty
p. 134: Doug Pensinger
p. 136: STF/AFP
p. 137: Robert Laberge
p. 139: National Baseball Hall of Fame Library/MLB Photos
p. 145: Bruce Bennett/Time Life Pictures
p. 146: Bruce Bennett Studios
p. 149: Bruce Bennett Studios
p. 151: John Dominis/Time Life Pictures
p. 152: Art Rickerby/Time Life Pictures
p. 155: David Cannon
p. 157: Rob Taggart
p. 158: Tony Duffy
p. 161: STF/AFP
p. 163: Bruce Bennett Studios
p. 165: Diamond Images
p. 166: Bruce Bennett Studios
p. 169: (left) Keeneland/Morgan Collection
p. 173: Jerome Delay/AFP
p. 175: (left) Mark Cardwell/AFP
p. 175: (right) Jerome Delay/AFP
p. 176: (left) Jacques Demarthon/AFP
p. 176: (right) Mladen Antonov/AFP
p. 179: Al Bello
p. 181: Al Bello
p. 182: Jeff Haynes/AFP
p. 185: (top) Peter Carvelli
p. 185: (bottom) Rusty Jarrett
p. 186: Robert Laberge
p. 189: Erik S. Lesser

AP/Wide World Photos
p. 21; p. 26; p. 27; p. 31; p. 51; p. 52; p. 54-55; p. 57; p. 67; p. 69; p. 70; p. 71; p. 75; p. 96-97; p. 99; p. 103; p. 105 (left); p. 106; p. 108-109; p. 113; p. 118; p. 133; p. 141; p. 142; p. 169(right); p. 171

The New York Public Library
p. 92; p. 95

ACKNOWLEDGMENTS

OFFEN SPORTSWRITERS CAN be sorts of rivals, but in this case it is a gathering of friends who have come together to help us create this book. Thanks first to my co-author David Fischer for his outstanding research and fine words. David and I called on several experts to help provide different viewpoints and styles, as well as insiders' knowledge. Their names are listed with the chapters they wrote and you can read a bit more about their backgrounds there. But thanks here to contributors Ted Keith, Jon Scher, John Walters, John Wiebusch, and Eric Zweig. Thanks to Jenna Free and her colleagues at becker&mayer!—Shayna Ian, Kasey Clark, Joanna Price, and Leah Finger—for bringing us onboard and keeping us honest.

Thanks most, of course, to the athletes who have thrilled us for years, whose intensity, whether in rivalries or not, has provided us with entertainment, joy, sorrow, excitement, and reflected glory, among many other things. As you'll see in the first chapter, my co-author and I are rivals a couple dozen times a year; the rest of the time we agree: Sports do not define our lives, but they would be sorely empty without them.

—J.B.